W9-CHK-022

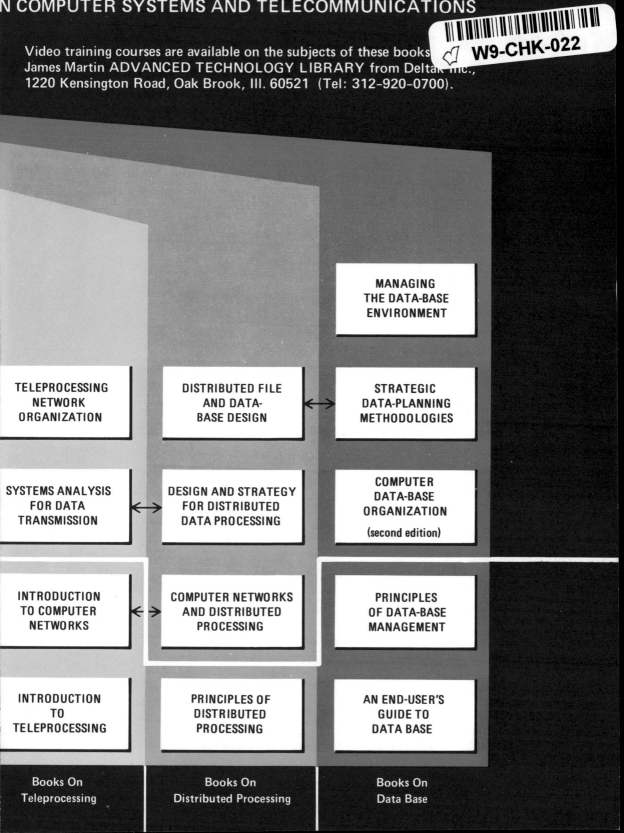

MANAGING
THE DATA-BASE
ENVIRONMENT

TELEPROCESSING
NETWORK
ORGANIZATION

DISTRIBUTED FILE
AND DATA-
BASE DESIGN

STRATEGIC
DATA-PLANNING
METHODOLOGIES

SYSTEMS ANALYSIS
FOR DATA
TRANSMISSION

DESIGN AND STRATEGY
FOR DISTRIBUTED
DATA PROCESSING

COMPUTER
DATA-BASE
ORGANIZATION

(second edition)

INTRODUCTION
TO COMPUTER
NETWORKS

COMPUTER NETWORKS
AND DISTRIBUTED
PROCESSING

PRINCIPLES
OF DATA-BASE
MANAGEMENT

INTRODUCTION
TO
TELEPROCESSING

PRINCIPLES OF
DISTRIBUTED
PROCESSING

AN END-USER'S
GUIDE TO
DATA BASE

Books On
Teleprocessing

Books On
Distributed Processing

Books On
Data Base

AN END-USER'S GUIDE TO DATA BASE

A *James Martin* BOOK

AN END-USER'S

GUIDE
TO DATA BASE

JAMES MARTIN

This book was written
with no technical words
except where they are unavoidable
and clearly explained.

PRENTICE-HALL, INC., Englewood Cliffs, New Jersey 07632

Library of Congress Cataloging in Publication Data

Martin, James
  An end-user's guide to data base.
   Includes bibliographical references and index.
   1. Data base management. I. Title.
QA76.9.D3M365 1981   001.64′2   80–27478
ISBN 0-13-277129-2

An End-User's Guide to Data Base
James Martin

Editorial/production supervision by
  Linda Mihatov Paskiet
Manufacturing buyers: *Joyce Levatino
  and Gordon Osbourne*

Printed in the United States of America

10 9 8 7 6 5 4

PRENTICE-HALL INTERNATIONAL, INC., *London*
PRENTICE-HALL OF AUSTRALIA PTY. LIMITED, *Sydney*
PRENTICE-HALL OF CANADA, LTD., *Toronto*
PRENTICE-HALL OF INDIA PRIVATE LIMITED, *New Delhi*
PRENTICE-HALL OF JAPAN, INC., *Tokyo*
PRENTICE-HALL OF SOUTHEAST ASIA PTE. LTD., *Singapore*
WHITEHALL BOOKS LIMITED, *Wellington, New Zealand*

A data base is a shared collection of interrelated data designed to meet the needs of multiple types of end users.

The data are stored so that they are independent of the programs which use them. A common and controlled approach is used in adding new data and modifying and retrieving existing data.

The objective of data-base technology is to speed up computer application development, reduce application maintenance costs, and provide end users with the data they need for doing their jobs as efficiently as possible.

Data-base technology will become the backbone of most data processing.

It is unlikely to succeed fully unless the end users it serves are intimately involved in certain aspects of its design.

TO CORINTHIA

CONTENTS

7   **How to Succeed with Data Modeling**   65

8   **Data-Base Languages for End Users**   75

PREFACE

As data-base technology spreads, it is desirable that certain principles of data-base systems should be understood by accountants, engineers, administrative managers, civil servants, shop-floor foremen, department heads, budget controllers, professionals, corporate presidents—in fact, all end users who will be affected by it.

Many of these end users have almost no knowledge of computers or software. This book is written for them. It omits any description of how data-base management systems work or other detailed technology. It concentrates on what end users have to know and do to survive and profit from the data-base environment.

Although it is a nontechnical book, it may be read by data-processing staff because it discusses what makes data-base installations succeed or fail. To a large extent success or disappointment is dependent on the end users—their involvement in the definition and logical modeling of the data, their employment of end-user data-base languages, and their acceptance of the results and the principle of shared data. Too many data-base managers become experts on the software and machine performance, but neglect the modeling of data and the end users' needs.

End users everywhere should understand the contents of this book. It can be taught to them in a one-day course; however, two days are recommended, with the users attempting to draw bubble charts and create simple models of **their own** data during the two days.

To obtain more understanding of the technology the reader might follow this book with the author's *Principles of Data-Base Management,* and to obtain more understanding of the management process, the author's *Managing the Data-Base Environment.* It is suggested that users and analysts watch the video courses made by the author with Deltak Inc., Oak Brook, Illinois, with the foregoing two titles. The video course "Managing the Data-Base Environment" explores in detail what has made data-base installations succeed or fail.

A supplementary manual, QUESTIONS AND ANSWERS TO AN END-USER'S GUIDE TO DATA BASE, is available from Prentice-Hall.

James Martin

AN END-USER'S
GUIDE
TO DATA BASE

A *James Martin* BOOK

1 WHAT IS DATA BASE?

INTRODUCTION Data-base technology is becoming increasingly important to data processing. Much data processing will be built on top of data bases in the future, so the existence of appropriate data bases will be vital to the running of corporations and other bodies.

Not all data-base systems have been a success. Many have failed to achieve the advantages that good data-base operation should bring. It has become clear in surveying the disappointments and the success stories that **effective involvement of the end users is critical for success.** To achieve this involvement there are certain things the users must understand about data-base technology. It is a new world for them and can be a bewildering one because of the complexity and jargon. Often, end users understand neither the principles of data base nor their own essential role in data-base evolution.

This book explains to users what they should know about data base, and what role they should play in its design and evolution. It does so without using the jargon words which make data-base technology appear complex. It is important that **all** end users comprehend the simple concepts that are described.

Many users have fears about the introduction of data-base systems. Their jobs will be changed by data-base usage. They are stepping into a dark room and cannot see where they are going. The best way to overcome the fear is to throw some light. This is achieved partly by understanding the principles described in this book, and partly by involvement in the data definition and design, as we will describe.

The term **end** user implies the **ultimate** user of a data-base facility, that is, not an interim user such as a programmer programming functions for the **end** users. Data-base end users are a diverse cross section of humanity: accountants, engineers, administrative managers, civil servants, shop-floor foremen, department heads, budget controllers, professionals, actuaries, the president and his aides.

Any manager, planner, or professional whose job will be changed in the future by data-base systems should understand what is in this book, and become involved.

WHAT IS A DATA BASE?

A data base is a collection of data which are shared and used for multiple purposes.

Any one user does not perceive all of the types of data in the data base, but only those that are needed for his or her job.* A user may perhaps perceive only one file of data. That file always has the same structure and appears simple, but in fact it is derived from a much more complex data structure. Other users see **different** files derived from the same data base.

A data base is thus not only shared by multiple users, but it is **perceived** differently by different users.

You might think of blind persons confronted with an elephant. One person touches its leg and perceives it as being like a tree trunk. One touches its tail and perceives it as being like a rope. Another touches its tusks, and so on. Similarly, different data-base users perceive different **views** of the data. Someone has to design the entire elephant. In doing so he must make sure that he meets the diverse needs of many users. In other words, all relevant user views must be derivable from the data base.

Data-base design is a complex task. The technical aspects of it can be largely automated. If this is done, the most difficult part of the task is understanding the data needed by the users, and representing it in the data base. This is made complicated by the fact that different users use different names for the same data item, and sometimes the same name for data items which are really different.

For computers to work correctly, a high degree of precision is needed in representing the data they use.

It is up to user departments to ensure that the data they need are truly represented in a corporation's data bases, correctly defined, appropriately organized, and protected from harm or invalid use. The data-base designer needs the user departments' help in understanding their data needs.

It is pleasant, now that the world of computers has become so complex, to let one's imagination drift back to the days of Dickens. In those days data processing was done by a clerk with a quill pen who was perched on a high stool and perhaps wearing a top hat. In front of him he had a set of thick and well-bound ledgers. If an order were made for a certain quantity of goods, a clerk would deal with this transaction in its entirety. He might look at his stock sheets to see whether the order could be fulfilled from stock or whether some of it had to be manufactured. He would update the order book, and if any goods were sent he would modify the stock sheets to make out a bill for the customer and made an entry on the appropriate page of a customer ledger—a simple process which was easy to understand.

If anyone had any query about the state of the business, about a certain item of stock, or about an outstanding debt of a customer, the clerk could turn to the appropriate pages of his ledgers and immediately produce the answer. One can imagine such a clerk today taking orders by telephone and answering queries over the

---

* In this book we use "his" and "he" as an abbreviation of "his or her" and "he or she."

telephone. He would balance his books at the end of each day, and if costing figures were required, he could maintain them so that they were as up to date as required.

However, admirable as the methods of the Dickensian clerk were, they could work only in a fairly small company. As the company grew, the size of the ledgers increased until several clerks were needed to maintain them. Division of labor made the job easier, and one clerk would maintain the stock sheets while another did the billing, and so forth. Earlier in this century various means for mechanization were introduced, and to make efficient use of them, the work was split up into batches. For example, several hundred transactions may have been grouped into a batch. One accounting function would be carried out on all the transactions by one clerk or one machine, and then the next function would be performed by another clerk or another machine.

When punched-card accounting was introduced, it became economical to have very large batches. Many trays of cards would be fed through one machine before the setup of that machine was changed for the next function it would perform. Similarly, with the use of magnetic tape on computers, large tape files would be processed with one program before the file was sorted and made ready for the next operation. In working this way the flexibility of the old clerical methods was lost. It was no longer possible to give one transaction individual treatment. It was no longer possible to give quick answers to inquiries about the status of an account, or the credit worthiness of a customer, or the amount of an item in stock. Or, at least, if such an inquiry was made, the answer might be a week or more out of date. When items were to be posted, it was necessary for the computer to read every item in the file as it scanned its way to the ones to be updated, and every item had often to be written out afresh on a new tape, whether it was updated or not.

Batch processing, with data rigidly divided into separate files for each application, was not the ideal way to operate. It would have been much more convenient for management to have all the information about running their organization up to date and at their fingertips. Because of the nature of data-processing techniques, management was living with a compromise. The compromise stayed in existence so long that it became the accepted method of operation, and little thought was given to its desirability.

The use of a data base is like having a superbly fast and brilliant Dickensian clerk who keeps data for many applications. He organizes his books so that minimum writing is necessary and so that he can search the books quickly to answer any queries that may come along. Unlike his pedestrian predecessors who could write or read items in only one ledger, he rushes from one set of data to another, collecting together separate items to respond to highly varied requests for information. He is a godsend to management.

Executives often need information which spans departments or spans traditional boundaries in the corporation, such as the engineering, accounting, personnel, production, and marketing functions. They need information on personnel implications of marketing decisions, or the impact on production of a new distribution strategy, or the labor costs associated with higher sales. Where each department has its own batch-processing operations, the computer is of little value in answering such questions. However, with a data-base approach the Dickensian super-clerk rushes from one department's books to another, searching and correlating the data. The structure of the data that are stored is agreed upon centrally so that interdepartmental usage is possible.

The data within a corporation (or other organization) will increasingly be regarded as a basic resource needed to run the corporation. As with other basic resources, professional management and organization of the data are needed. The importance of efficient use of data for production control, marketing, accounting, planning, and other functions will become so great in a computerized corporation that it will have a major effect on the growth and survival of corporations in a competitive marketplace. In government departments and the massive data factories of modern man, the Dickensian super-clerks will make the difference between data being used efficiently, facilitating delicate control mechanisms, and data being a labor-consuming encumbrance of sluggish bureaucracy.

VALUE OF DATA   The value of data depends on the uses to which they are put. Often today, data needed in an important decision-making process exist somewhere in an organization in a machine-readable form but are not available to the decision makers when they need them. Furthermore, the cost of producing new computer programs and modifying old ones is often extraordinarily high because the data are not in the right form. To make data as useful as possible and to control system development cost, appropriate design of data systems is necessary. Decision makers can have far better information than they had before computers, and they can have it immediately when they need it. However, the task of building up the information sources is complex, and many managers have underestimated the difficulties and time involved.

A corporation will have various different collections of data for different purposes in different locations. They may be linked by telecommunications to the machines or people who employ them. They can differ widely in their structure.

In earlier data processing one or more "files" of records were kept for each application. The intention of a data base is to allow the same collection of data to be shared and to serve as many applications as is useful. Hence, a data base is often conceived of as the repository of information needed for running certain functions in a body such as a corporation, factory, university, or government department. Such a data base permits not only the retrieval of data but also the continuous modification of data needed for the control of operations. It may be possible to "search" the data base to obtain answers to queries or information for planning purposes. The collection of data may serve several departments, often cutting across political boundaries.

In the much publicized dream of a data base, a corporation, or other organization, keeps all its data in a large reservoir in which a diversity of data users can go fishing. Such a data base would be highly complex, and in general the dream is far from being achieved in reality. A complex data base has to be built up stage by stage. In reality, today most data bases serve a varied, but limited, set of applications. One computer may use multiple different data bases.

A major task for most corporations is to decide what data bases they need, where they are best located, what data should be stored in them, and how they should be organized. Large progressive corporations already store a gigantic amount of information in their computer storage units but need to organize it better. The amount of data stored will increase drastically, and the ways the data are organized will be fundamentally changed to increase their usefulness.

Critical to the whole subject is understanding how the end users employ data. The data for a computerized corporation need to be cleanly thought out, consistent among different users, and structured in a fashion which is as stable as possible. There are formal techniques for doing this. They need thorough involvement of the end users.

2 PRODUCTIVITY AND FLEXIBILITY

INTRODUCTION   There is one story after another in data processing of management not being able to obtain the information they need from their computer system.

One story in the *Harvard Business Review* (1) describes a marketing vice-president confronted with sales forecasts for a new line of industrial products, similar to the company's existing line. The new line was intended to complement the existing line, where competition had been making serious inroads. The forecasts for the new line were more promising than the marketing vice-president had dared to hope, and the forecasting team had shown good reason to take them seriously.

To gain the much-needed profits from the increased sales it was necessary to ensure that the higher sales volume could be manufactured and distributed. Data were needed about plant capacity, personnel, and warehouses. A preliminary examination indicated that the regional warehousing facilities might impose a severe constraint on sales, both in physical space and manpower. The forecasts, however, did not show regional variations in sales in such a way as to make it clear which warehouses would be worst hit and which ones nearby might have excess capacity.

The marketing vice-president had planned an aggressive promotion campaign, and he suspected that if it were successful some regions would need four times their normal warehousing capacity for at least three months. The chief executive officer concluded that it was essential to compute in more detail the impact of the projected marketing campaign on inventory turnover and warehouse crowding. He assumed that this could be computed because the computer already had

1. Inventory simulation programs and several years' data on inventory turnover.

2. Forecasting programs designed to produce forecast sales reports by region and product.

3. A model for market penetration of the new line based on the sales of the old line which it would supplement.

The chief executive officer presented his requirement to the data-processing (DP) manager. The results, he said, were needed quickly because the new product line was only a few months from announcement. The DP manager pointed out that, unfortunately, while the data needed did exist, they were not in a form which could be used for the required simulation. The programs for forecasting sales did provide regional projections, but the resulting records did not contain the data necessary for regional inventory simulations. Further, the data about past years' sales were specially coded for the programs with which they had been used in the past and could not be used by the regional inventory simulations without a massive reorganization.

> The Chief Executive Officer looked glum: "How long will it take you to clean up the data and write a simulation program that will give us some answers?"
> "Nine months, maybe a year," said the DP manager.
> "Because all our data are frozen into these other programs?" the CEO asked.
> "That's the main reason," the DP manager replied.
> "That's a hell of a reason," the CEO said and stalked toward the door.
> "Of course, we could have done it the other way," the DP manager called after him, "but now what we'd have to do is. . . ."
> But he was gone. (1)

"The other way" would have used data-base techniques instead of letting each department use files designed solely for its own purposes—but it was too late.

MULTIPLE USAGE OF DATA
Figure 2.1 illustrates the way data are organized for computers which do not use data-base techniques. There are many files of records, some on tape and some on quickly accessible media such as disk. The records contain data items, shown as circles in Fig. 2.1. When a program is written for a new application or a variation of an old application, there may be a file which contains the required set of data items. Often, however, there is not, and a new file has to be created.

Suppose that a new user request needs a file with data items A, F, and H. These data items do not appear together in the existing files in Fig. 2.1. Other files must be sorted and merged to obtain the new file, but this will not be straightforward if, as with the marketing problem above, the existing files do not have the required sets of keys. There may not be an H data item for every pair of A and F data items.

PROBLEMS WITH FILE SYSTEMS
There are three problems about the organization of data in **files** as in Fig. 2.1. To understand them the reader should imagine hundreds or thousands of files rather than the seven in Fig. 2.1.

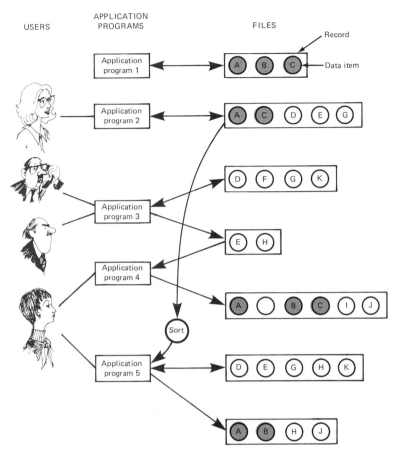

Figure 2.1 A file environment. For each new application a programmer or analyst creates a new file. A large installation has hundreds or thousands of such files with much redundancy of data.

First, *there is a high level of redundancy*. The same type of data item is stored in many different places. The different versions of the same data items may be in different stages of update. In other words, they have different values. This may give the appearance of inconsistency to users. A manager obtains a report saying one thing and a terminal inquiry says something different.

With multiple different copies of the same data item it is difficult to maintain consistency or to ensure integrity of the data items.

Second, *a file system is **inflexible.*** Requests for information which require data items to be grouped in different ways cannot be answered quickly. Most **ad hoc** queries from a user employing a generalized query language cannot be answered. Although the data exist, information cannot be provided relating to those data. The data cannot be processed in new ways without restructuring.

One sometimes hears the protest from management: "We paid millions for that computer system and we cannot obtain the information we want from it."

Third, *it can be expensive to make changes to a file system.*

Suppose that application program 3 in Fig. 2.1 has to be changed in such a way that its record [(E) (H)] has to be modified. Unfortunately, application program 4 uses this same record; therefore, application program 4 has to be modified. Many other application programs may also use the same record (Fig. 2.2) and all have to be changed.

A seemingly trivial change in a file environment sets off a chain reaction of other changes which have to be made. This upheaval is expensive and the necessary

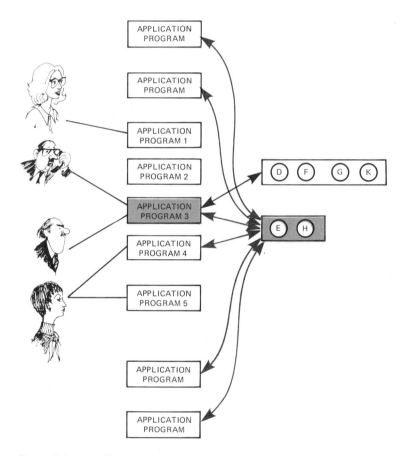

Figure 2.2 One file becomes used by multiple applications. When an application is changed (application program 3 above) and its file has to be restructured, then all the programs which use that file have to be changed. A seemingly trivial change in a file environment can set off a chain reaction of other changes which have to be made.

programmers are doing other work. Sometimes the modifications are difficult to make because the applications were not adequately documented.

As time goes on, this problem becomes worse because more and more programs are created. More programs have to be changed whenever a file is changed.

MAINTENANCE   Computer data in an organization are no more a static entity than are the contents of the organization's filing cabinets. The details of data stored, and the way they are used, change continuously. If a computer system attempts to impose an unchangeable file structure on an organization, it is doomed to the types of pressure that will result in most of the programming efforts being spent on modifying existing programs rather than developing new applications.

Figure 2.3 shows how programming costs have tended to change in organizations. The total programming costs in a typical organization have grown, becoming a higher proportion of the total data-processing budget. However, the programming worker-hours spent on new applications have fallen steadily. The reason is that the effort to maintain or modify the existing programs becomes greater and greater. It is often thought by systems analysts and data-processing managers that existing programs which work well can be left alone. In reality, however, the data which they create or use are needed for other applications and almost always needed in a slightly different form. New data-item types are added. New record types are needed with data-item types from several previous records. The data must be indexed in a different way. The physical layout of data is improved. Data bases for different applications are merged, and so forth.

The term **maintenance** is used to refer to the rewriting of old programs to make them conform to new data structures, new operating systems, terminals, and

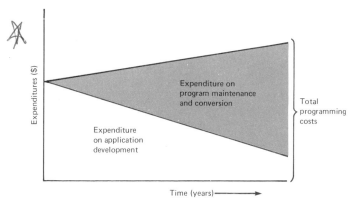

Figure 2.3   New application progress is often deferred by the rising cost of modifying existing programs and files. Some corporations now spend more than 80% of their programming budget just keeping current and only 20% forging ahead.

other system changes. Maintenance, if not consciously controlled, tends to rise as the number of programs grows. In some corporations it has risen to the disastrous level of 80% of the programming budget.

One of the main objectives of a data-base system is that new programs using the data in a modified form should be able to do so without having any effect on programs which use the same data in their old form. Furthermore, a program may be modified, changing in some way the data it uses, without disturbing any other programs which use those same data. In other words, **each program should be insulated** from the effects of changes to other programs, and all programs should be insulated from the effects of reorganizing the data.

Data-base systems attempt to lower the maintenance costs by separating the records which the programmers perceive from the records which are physically stored. You might think of the programmer as perceiving a **make-believe** record— a record which does not exist in physical reality. The data-base management software derives this record for the programmer from the collection of data which is physically stored.

Figure 2.4 illustrates this. In Fig. 2.4, when programmer 2 changes his record

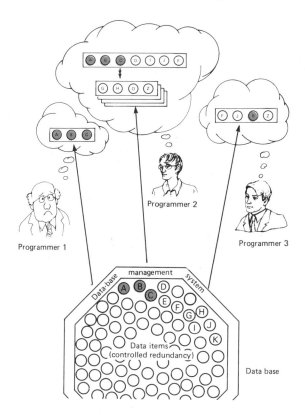

Figure 2.4 The programmers can live in blissful ignorance of how the data are really stored.

structure, his new record structure is derived from the data base by the data-base management system. The change made by programmer 1 does not force programmers 2 and 3 to change **their** records.

The make-believe records shown in Fig. 2.4 are called **logical** records. Each program refers to logical records, not the physical records which are stored in magnetic pulses on the disks or other storage media.

**DATA-BASE
MANAGEMENT
SYSTEMS**
The data-base management system is the entity which provides programmers or end users with the data they ask for. Like a conjurer pulling different-colored handkerchiefs out of a hat, it derives its users' **make-believe** records from its store of data. It finds out what **physical** records contain the data in a given request, has a means of locating those records, and from them derives the logical records that were asked for.

All the major computer manufacturers provide data-base management systems with names such as IMS, IDS, DMS, and IDMS (I in these names stands for Information or Integrated, D for Data, M for Management, and S for System). Independent software companies have also provided data-base management systems with names such as TOTAL, ADABAS, IDMS, and SYSTEM 2000.

It is generally not necessary for the end users to know how these products work. The reader can obtain more easy-to-read details of the technology from the author's book, *Principles of Data-Base Management*.

**ARE YOUR PROGRAMS
DATA-INDEPENDENT?**
A data base is intended to make data independent of the programs that use them. Either data or programs can be changed without causing the other to have to be changed. The data can be easily reorganized or their content added to. Old application programs do not have to be rewritten when changes are made to data structures, data layout, or the physical devices on which data are stored.

This independence of data is essential if data are to become a general-purpose corporate resource. In the past, data structures have been devised by a programmer for his own use. He writes a program to create a file of data. Usually, when another programmer needs the data for another purpose it is not structured in the way he wants, so he creates another file—hence the duplication in Fig. 2.1.

Data independence is one of the most important differences between the way data are organized in data bases and the way they are organized in the file systems of computers that do not use data-base management software. The programmers can each have their own logical data structure, as shown in Fig. 2.4, and can program in blissful ignorance of how the data are really organized. When the data organization is changed, **the old programs still work.**

This facility makes the data-base software complex. However, without it, new application development can be immensely time-consuming and prohibitively expensive because it makes it necessary to rewrite existing programs or convert existing data. The total number of worker-years that a corporation has invested in application programs grows steadily. The programmers are long since gone, and it is too late to complain that their documentation is inadequate.

The greater the number of programs, the more horrifying the thought of having to convert them or their data, so there is reluctance in the DP department to respond to the latest needs of the end users.

AD HOC REQUESTS   New, unanticipated requests for information, such as that in the story at the start of this chapter, are increasing. As end-user management realizes the potential value of the data that are stored, their requests for information increase. Much future growth can be expected in the data requests from users as they better comprehend the potential of computers. However, to the data-processing manager without appropriate data bases, these requests can be a menace. He does not have the programmers to deal with the requests. Many end users in a file environment are finding that important requests for data or reports are not met.

The concept of data base, shown in Fig. 2.5, if it works as intended, should enable the DP department to be more responsive to such requests. However, for this to happen the right **logical** data structures must be created, and this requires close cooperation between the data-base designer and the end users.

In the organization of Fig. 2.5, the data items are pooled to form a data base with software that can extract any combination of data items that a programmer wishes. In reality the data items are usually not stored entirely in isolation, as suggested by Fig. 2.5, but in groups of related data items, sometimes called **records,** sometimes **segments.** The software may be able to extract segments and combine them to form the records that an application program uses.

Another important feature shown in Fig. 2.5, at the bottom, is the data-base interrogation software. This enables some users of the data to interact directly with the data base without application programs having to be written. Instead, the user employs a dialogue at a terminal, or possibly fills in a form, to express his needs.

Data-base dialogues for end users are becoming increasingly important. They enable information to be extracted from computers, and reports and listings generated **without** programming. Increasingly, end users will interact directly with the data-base systems. This is discussed in Chapter 8.

Figure 2.5 suggests that a corporation's data are stored in a large reservoir in which the users can go fishing. Although this figure forms a useful way to explain data-base concepts to management, it is nevertheless a naive view of a data base—in some cases dangerously naive, as we shall see. The data items inside the octagon of Fig. 2.5 have to be organized in such a way that they can be found and accessed with sufficient speed. The organizing introduces many complexities into data-base design. The structuring problems can be sufficiently great that a designer may sometimes elect to employ separate data-base systems, even though they contain much of the same information.

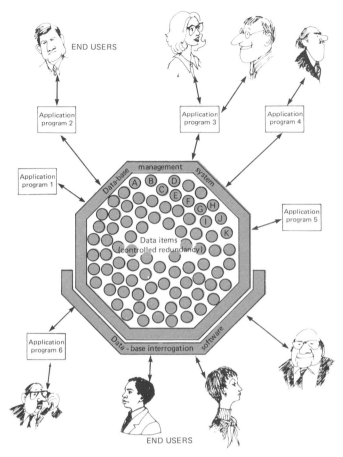

Figure 2.5 Application programs derive their logical records from the data base, and end users gain direct access to the data base with high-level data-base languages (Chapter 8).

The "reservoir" concept of management information systems, or other information systems, is much easier to conceive than to implement. It is proving a very complex and lengthy operation to build up such data bases, and with current hardware it is expensive to search them sufficiently quickly to give real-time answers to unanticipated queries.

The striving for flexibility, however, is vital. In many corporations, systems (of accounts, organization, methods, responsibilities, and procedures) have been more of a hindrance to change than physical plant and unamortized capital investments. For some, retraining the whole labor force would be easier than changing the system. Quite frequently, the computer has contributed to the inflexibility by dressing hallowed procedures in a rigid electronic framework. The computer has been hailed as one of the most versatile and flexible machines ever built, but in many corporations, because of the difficulty and cost of changing their programs and data bases, it becomes a straitjacket which precludes change and even constrains corporate policy. The comment is often heard, "We cannot do that because change is too difficult with our computer system."

One of the most difficult tricks that we have to learn is how to introduce automation without introducing rigidity. The computer industry is only now beginning to glimpse how that can be done. Data-base techniques are an important part of the answer.

CONSTANT CHANGE   One of the most important characteristics of data processing is the planning for constant change. Dynamic restructuring of the data base must be possible as new types of data and new applications are added. The restructuring should be possible without having to rewrite the application programs, and in general should cause as little upheaval as possible. The ease with which a data base can be changed will have a major effect on the rate at which data-processing applications can be developed in a corporation.

It is often easy for a systems analyst to imagine that the data structure he has designed for an application represents its ultimate content and usage. He leaves some spare characters in the records and thinks that these will accommodate any change that will occur. Consequently, he ties his data to a physical organization which is efficient for that particular structure. Time and time again he is proven wrong. The requirements change in unforeseen ways. The data structures have to be modified, and consequently many application programs have to be rewritten and debugged. The larger an installation's base of application programs, the more expensive is this process.

As we commented, 80% of the programming budget is being spent on maintaining or modifying past programs and data in some installations. This ratio is extremely inhibiting to the development of data processing in the organization. It is desirable to write today's programs in such a way that the same ratio will not apply five years hence. If we continue to write programs without data independence, the maintenance difficulties will grow worse as the numbers of programs grow, until the impact cripples the capability to take advantage of the new hardware and techniques that are now under development.

FAILURE   The decade ahead is likely to be an era of great invention in the techniques for storing and organizing data, and many of the new techniques will be highly complex. The greater the rate of introduction of new techniques or modified data organizations, the greater is the need to protect the application programs and programmers from them. This is one of the main reasons why we need data-base systems rather than merely file systems without the data independence.

However, many data-base installations have failed to lower the maintenance costs and failed to respond to end users as needed. The main reason has been that the data structures represented in the data base have not been appropriate.

To achieve data structures which are satisfactory, careful modeling of the data is needed, as described later in this report. This modeling process needs a high degree of involvement by the end users.

DELUSIONS   There are several common misconceptions about database systems which need clarifying.

First, a data base, or data-base management system, does not imply a "management information system." There is no direct relationship between the terms. In their initial use, most data bases should be thought of merely as a way of storing data for conventional applications and making that data more easily accessible to end users. Data-base techniques are justified by giving faster application development, lowering the cost of maintenance, and enabling much end-user data to be obtained without programming. They permit the data-processing department to be responsive. One type of application of data base is the providing of information to management.

A second delusion is that a data-base system is sometimes described as containing all the data items in a corporation or a division. Typical comments on the subject from journals such as the *Harvard Business Review* include the following misconception: "If the company had maintained all its computer-readable data in a single pool or bank—in a so-called 'data base'—and if the company had structured this base of data so that a program for virtually any feasible use could have been run from this data base, then it would have been a matter of sheer expertise and flair for a good, experienced programmer to concoct a program that pulled the desired information together" (2). And "The data-base concept structures EDP activity in such a way that all of a company's computer-readable data are merged in a single pool, which is used to run both routine programs and programs written in response to ad hoc requests" (2).

Any attempt to implement so grand a notion is doomed to disaster before it begins. One of the reasons for data-base techniques is that files or data bases that were separate can later be combined. In this way, larger collections of data can be built up with a subsequent drop in data redundancy and increase in data-base interrogation capability. However, to begin with the notion that the data base will serve everyone who uses data is asking for trouble.

Related to the foregoing delusion is the notion that an organization will have **one** data base. In reality it is likely to have many data bases, eventually perhaps hundreds. Many different data bases may be used on the same data-base system, but they will be both physically and logically separate. They should be built with a common schema language and common design policies because linkages between them will be forged in the future. The data-base management system should be common to all, but the data bases themselves entirely separate.

INFRASTRUCTURE   A better way to think of data-base systems is that they form an infrastructure which will allow better use of data processing in the future. If the principles of this book are followed, they force clear thinking about data. A clearly defined representation of the corporate data, modeled in a relatively stable form, will steadily grow. This data modeling should keep well ahead of the implementation of specific data bases. The implementation will be such that the data representation can change and grow without usually forcing the rewriting of application programs. The programs will not have to be rewritten when better hardware is installed.

At today's state of the art, then, most corporations should not talk about a corporate-wide data base but rather a **corporate-wide organizing principle** which forms the structure for data-base development. An essential of this principle is that the data descriptions and data dictionary be standardized throughout the corporation.

INCREMENTAL GROWTH   The growth which the infrastructure permits should have two characteristics. First, it should be planned, insofar as is possible. Although planning is desirable, it must be recognized that a data base will inevitably be used in ways which were not anticipated when it was designed. Second, the plan should involve small incremental steps, one application or one improvement to be implemented at a time on each data base.

The first applications selected for use with a data base should involve three characteristics. First, the data base should not be too complicated. Second, the application should be one which is clearly cost-justifiable. And third, **the management of the user departments should give full support and cooperation.**

As the data in a corporation is defined and modeled (as described later) more separate data bases come into existence. When more data bases exist, more projects are undertaken using these data bases. Many such projects may go on at the same time. Most projects using the data bases will be relatively short in duration—not more than a few months. Many of the incremental steps will be very short to implement, such as the production of a new type of report from an existing data base.

After several years of stage-by-stage buildup the overall data-base systems will begin to look impressive if they were appropriately directed toward overall goals. To be successful the data-base management system used must provide a high level of data independence, so that growth in the structure of the data base can continue without rewriting programs.

Unfortunately, although this stage-by-stage buildup is the best formula for success, an organization-wide all-embracing implementation sometimes appears more attractive to systems analysts or to management. Few projects for a grandiose data-base-to-end-all-data-bases have met with other than bitter disappointment. If grandiose plans are needed, they should be for a standardized corporate-wide framework within which data bases evolve and interlink a stage at a time.

18

Great cities are not built in one monolithic implementation. They grow and evolve and are the sum of many smaller pieces of work. If their structure can be planned so that the piecemeal implementations fit into an overall design, then they will be more workable cities.

The stage-by-stage buildup of a computerized corporation requires good forward-looking planning of what should be in the data bases. The end users have a vital role in helping the data administrator create data bases which are stable and permit stage-by-stage application development. If stable data bases are not created (as described in Chapters 5 through 7), then when new applications come along they cannot use the existing data; new data are created for them and the concept of shared subject data bases disintegrates into a free-for-all with each application going its own way and eventually resulting in the maintenance problems illustrated in Fig. 2.2.

3 WHO DOES WHAT?

INTRODUCTION   The major difference between data-base operation and file operation is that a high degree of sharing of data takes place.

This has several effects. It means that the design and management of data spans multiple departments which may previously have kept their data to themselves. It raises questions in the end users' minds about who owns the data, whether the data are private, and whether anyone could harm or invalidate the data. (These questions are addressed in Chapter 9.) It means that users from separate departments must cooperate, first at a high level to determine what data resources are needed, and second at a low level to define the data items and data structures.

A move from a file environment to a data-base environment is not just a change in software; it is a change in management. Without an appropriate change in management, data-base technology will not truly succeed.

LEVELS OF   The sharing of data takes place at several levels, as
DATA SHARING   shown in Figs. 3.1 through 3.3.

At the lowest level (Fig. 3.1) the same data item (field) is used in multiple records or documents.

At the next level (Fig. 3.2) the same files or data-item groupings are used in multiple applications.

Multiple groups of data items are organized into data bases. One system may contain several separate data bases. One such data base might contain all the data about customers, or all the data about parts, and so on. At the highest level of sharing (Fig. 3.3), each complete data base may be used by several departments, divisions, or other organizational entities.

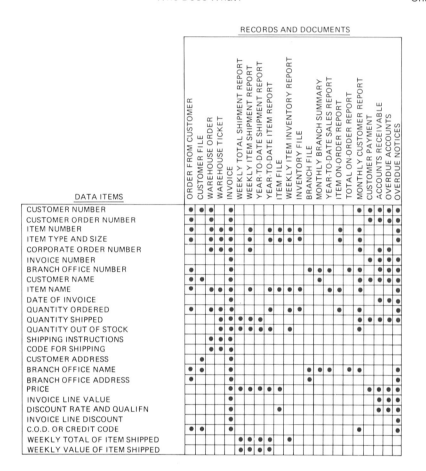

Figure 3.1 The same data items are used in multiple records and documents.

DATA-ITEM DEFINITION

For all levels of sharing, agreement must be established on the definitions and representation of each data item.

The types of data items that are used in a corporation have to be given names and must be defined. Many corporations are in the process of building a **dictionary** specifying and standardizing the types of data items in their corporate data bases. In a payroll application the data items have names such as GROSS MONTHLY PAY, FEDERAL INCOME TAX DEDUCTION, EMPLOYEE NAME, and SOCIAL SECURITY NUMBER. In a purchasing application they have names such as SUPPLIER NUMBER, SUPPLIER NAME, INVOICE DATE, QUANTITY ORDERED, and so forth. As the desire to analyze the corporate activity develops—a natural by-product of computer usage—more elaborate data items are needed, such as QUANTITY OF DELIVERIES LATE

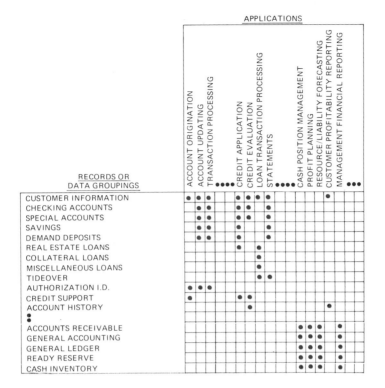

Figure 3.2   The same files or data groupings are used in multiple applications.

YEAR-TO-DATE FROM THIS SUPPLIER. Large corporations have more than 10,000 data items, with the number still growing rapidly.

Different computer applications, serving different departments of the corporation, can share many of the same data items, an employee's name, a part number, a customer order, and the details of these need not be separately recorded for each different department that uses them (as they have been in the past). They can be recorded once in a standard fashion and the data organized in such a way that they can be used for many different purposes.

The standardization and definition of this large number of data items is a lengthy operation and is made longer because different departments often define the same item differently or disagree about its precise meaning. Many corporations have not yet reached the stage of standardizing the corporate data items, but this is an essential step toward building up the data bases they will eventually need.

One corporation which is spending considerable effort on standardizing the definitions of its data items writes as follows:

> Common records at each location will increase our effectiveness in . . . interpreting and assisting with another plant's problems . . . transferring or promoting personnel to other locations . . . transferring product responsibilities

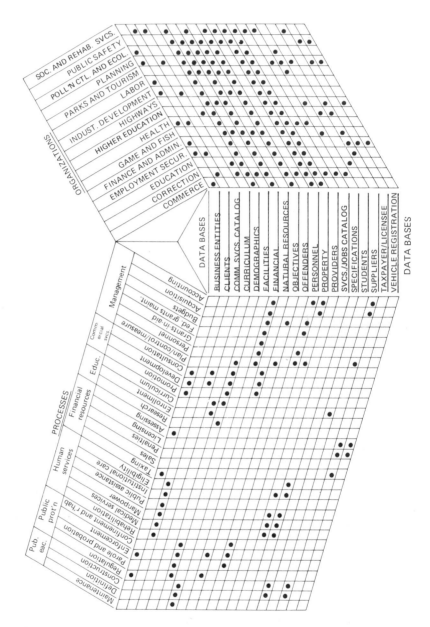

Figure 3.3 An efficiently planned set of data bases may be shared by multiple processes and multiple organizational groups. It should therefore cut across political boundaries. This example is taken from a local government study (3).

24

... exchanging product information ... starting up new plants. ... Will be of great significance to new people joining the company. ... It will be easier for personnel to exchange information when that information has a common meaning. ... Other areas of interplant communications will be substantially improved ... faster, more accurate communications ... faster response to changing conditions ... shorter lead times ... improved performance at lower cost ... will result. (4)

The difficulties of linking together or integrating the data base, and of standardizing the data items, can be particularly acute in a corporation with several divisions or plants, which have each evolved their own ways of keeping accounting, engineering, sales, production, or other data. In some corporations the struggle for standardization of computer-processable data will go on for many years.

DATA MODELING   Data items do not exist in isolation but are associated with one another. Maps need to be drawn of which data items are associated with which others, and what types of association these are. Such maps give an overall representation of the data that is needed to run an organization. They are referred to as data models.

Modeling the data is fundamental to successful data-base operation. In many data-base installations it has not been done adequately and the full advantages of data base are consequently not achieved. It is discussed in subsequent chapters.

Data definition and modeling go hand in hand and are independent of any one application, any current implementation, or any specific computer or software. They are fundamental to the process of understanding the data in a corporation.

DATA ADMINISTRATOR   The person who presides over the process of defining and modeling the data is called a **data administrator.**

To accomplish the task, the data administrator needs to work closely with the end users. The best way to do this is to set up a **user group** for the creation of a particular data base. The users, systems analysts, and the data administrator create separate views of the data that are needed. An individual view might relate to a document, an inquiry, a report, or an application of the data. The separate views are synthesized into a common data model from which any of the views can be derived (Chapter 5).

The model and the definitions of data are reviewed periodically with the user group. There is usually substantial argument about the definitions of data. Agreement needs to be established about common definitions and data structures before the data can be put into a shared data base which can serve multiple users as effectively as possible.

Particularly important in modeling is to create a model which is **stable** so that old programs do not have to be rewritten when the data are employed in new ways. Tools and techniques are available for stable data modeling.

DATA-BASE DESIGNER

The task of physically designing the data base is different in nature from the task of data modeling, and is often done by a different person. Physical data-base design is concerned with the machine and data-base software. Data modeling is concerned with what data are needed to make the business function.

We will refer to the person who does the physical data-base design as the data-base **designer.** He needs to be a skilled technician who understands the subtleties of the data-base management system, and how to obtain good performance from it.

LOGICAL AND PHYSICAL DATA

The form in which the data are actually stored does not necessarily resemble the form in which they are presented to the application program. The end user's or application programmer's view of the data may be much simpler than the actual data and tailored to his own application. The data structure which the user or application program employs is referred to as a **logical** structure. The data structure, which is actually stored on tape, disks, or other media, is called a **physical** structure. The words **logical** and **physical** will be used to describe various aspects of data, **logical** always referring to the way the programmer or end user sees it and **physical** always referring to the way the data are recorded on the storage medium. The programmers' views illustrated in Fig. 2.4 are **logical** (make-believe views).

The difference between logical and physical records had a humble beginning. When records were first stored on tape, the **gap** between records was long compared with the records themselves. The gaps wasted much space, so it was economical to have lengthy physical records. Many logical records were therefore grouped into one physical record. The software separated them when they were presented to an application program and combined them when they were written on tape.

Today, the differences between logical and physical data can be much more complex. The linkages among data are often different in the programmer's view and in the physical organization (for example, the linkage between a factory PART record and a record for the SUPPLIER who supplies that part). We use the terms **logical relationship** and **logical data description** to describe the programmer's view. **Physical relationship** and **physical data description** describe actual ways in which data are stored. It is a function of the software to convert from the programmer's or user's logical statements and descriptions to the physical reality and back again.

Figure 3.4 shows an example of different logical and physical structure. Physical records on a disk contain logical records which are **chained** together; that is, a pointer in one logical record links it to another. The programmer requires a file of logical records in the sequence of the chain. He does not necessarily know about the chain. The software presents his program with logical records in the required sequence. Other programs may be given records in a different sequence. Many different types of data structures are possible.

The data model which the data administrator creates is entirely a **logical** structure of data. The data-base designer converts this **logical** structure into **physical** structures. The end users generally need not be concerned with the physical structures.

26

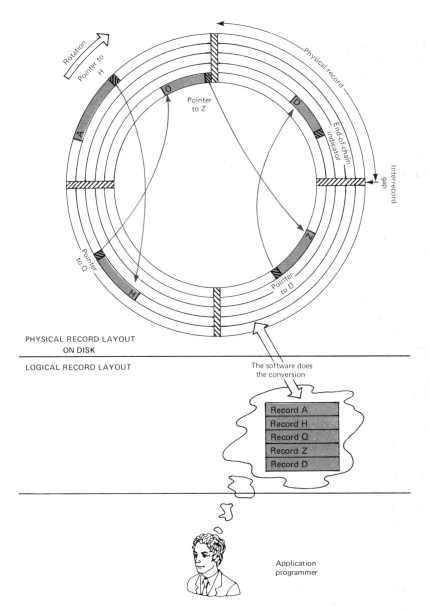

PHYSICAL RECORD LAYOUT
ON DISK

LOGICAL RECORD LAYOUT

Figure 3.4 An example of the difference between logical and physical records.

THE DESIGN
PROCESS

Figure 3.5 summarizes the design process.

The **data administrator** collects the data requirements expressed by end users and systems analysts, and synthesizes these to create a **logical** model of the data needed to run given activities. The model and definition of data items should be reviewed by a carefully selected committee of end users (labeled "end-user group" in Fig. 3.5) to achieve agreement on the definitions and to ensure as far as possible that no important data have been forgotten.

The data modeling process is fundamental to building a corporation automated with networks and data bases. It can be done independently of specific data-base design and should keep well ahead of the implementation of data bases for particular applications. Many corporations have not done the data modeling adequately, with the result that their data-base implementation degenerates into something more like **file** implementation than true data-base management. This causes problems like those discussed in Chapter 2.

The **data-base designer** creates specific data bases with specific software, implementing a selected part of the data model. He assists the programmers in efficient use of the data base. He monitors the resulting system and times the data base physically to achieve the best performance he can.

In many corporations where data-base technology has been a major success, the data modeling and the design of specific data bases have been done by different people, as shown in Fig. 3.5. In some successful installations the modeling and data-base design are done by the same person.

The personality and skills needed for creating corporate data models are different from those needed for specific data-base design. The data administrator needs skill with people and the ability to understand the business. The data-base designer needs skill with machines and software, and a knowledge of the complex mechanisms of the data-base management system.

The **end-user group** of Fig. 3.5 is particularly important. This committee of end users should be carefully chosen from the different areas represented by the model. It has the vital task of ensuring that end-user needs in general are met in the modeling process. It is up to end users to ensure that the data bases being created do in fact contain what they need and will need in the future. We discuss this process in subsequent chapters.

SUBJECT DATA BASES As we look back now on years of data-base case histories we can observe two types of approach: **application data bases** and **subject data bases.** It is quite clear which has given the best results **in the long term:** subject data bases.

Subject data bases relate to organizational **subjects** rather than to conventional computer **applications.** There should, for example, be a PRODUCT data base rather than separate INVENTORY, ORDER ENTRY, and QUALITY CONTROL data bases relating to that product. Many applications may then use the same data base. The development of new applications relating to that data base becomes easier than if application-oriented data bases had been built.

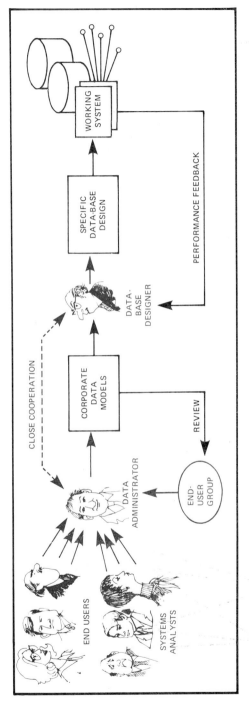

Figure 3.5   The data modeling and data-base design process.

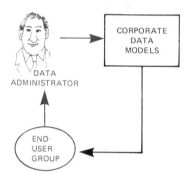

Figure 3.6   The end-user group.

Typical **subjects** for which data bases are built in a corporation are:

• PRODUCTS
• CUSTOMERS
• PARTS
• VENDORS
• ORDERS
• ACCOUNTS
• PERSONNEL
• DOCUMENTS
• ENGINEERING DESIGN

Figure 3.3 listed a set of **subject** data bases which are usable by many applications.

Some applications use more than one subject data base. The programs make **calls** to multiple separate data bases. For example:

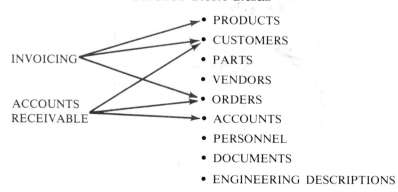

SUBJECT DATA BASES

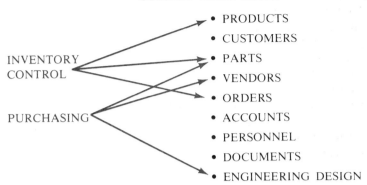

By using **subject** data bases rather than **applications** data bases the eventual number of data bases is far lower. A corporation builds up a very large number of applications but does not have a large number of operational **subjects.** If **files** are designed for specific applications, the number of files grows almost as rapidly as the number of applications, and results in the great proliferation of redundant data found in a typical tape library today. Application-oriented data bases can also proliferate rapidly. Using **subject** data bases, however, the number of applications grows much faster than the number of data bases, as shown in Fig. 3.7. Eventually, most new applications can be implemented rapidly because the data are available and the software provides tools to manipulate it. Indeed, many of the corporations

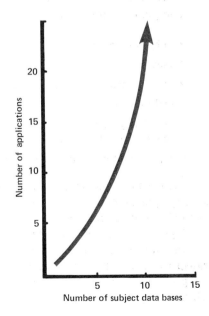

Figure 3.7 The rate of application development increases as the number of subject data bases increases. This curve was taken from a corporation with five years of **subject** data-base development.

that have successfully installed subject-oriented data bases have found that the curve in Fig. 3.7 grows so rapidly that they run out of computer power!

Clearly, the largest data-base systems are going to need very powerful complexes of computers in the future.

Some installations have created separate data bases for separate applications. This is easier and quicker than doing the overall design that is needed for subject data bases. However, as the years go by they end up with almost as many separate data bases as they would have had **files** if they had not used data-base management. They do not then achieve the advantages of data base described in Chapter 2. The use of data-base management in such installations has not reduced the program maintenance cost as it should.

THE VIEW FROM THE TOP

Many corporations have a top-level steering committee which makes decisions about major computer purchases and projects. Top end-user management participate in this process.

Often the steering committee does not plan the data-base requirements, but it is becoming increasingly important that this should be done. We will refer to the top-level data-base planner as the **data strategist**. He is sometimes called an *Information Resources Planner*. He should create a corporate-wide plan for what data resources are needed.

Figure 3.3 illustrates one such plan. This illustration includes only data bases. In fact, an organization is likely to have many existing **files.** It will also have collections of data for specific purposes such as certain end-user information systems. These need to be in the overall data resources plan.

The plan should include:

- Subject data bases
- Files
- Files in small distributed systems which relate to data bases elsewhere
- Old files which have to be converted
- Old (badly designed) data bases which have to be converted—often narrowly conceived application data bases
- Separate information systems (Chapter 11)

Increasingly, the data storage in a corporation is **distributed;** it exists at multiple geographical locations. The top-level plan should be concerned with what data bases exist at different sites, and to what extent they share the same data structures.

Figure 3.8 illustrates the high-level planning of data resources.

In some organizations the persons shown as **data administrator** and **data strategist** in Fig. 3.8 are the same person. Large organizations may have one data strategist with a view of the whole organization, and multiple data administrators, each handling different areas.

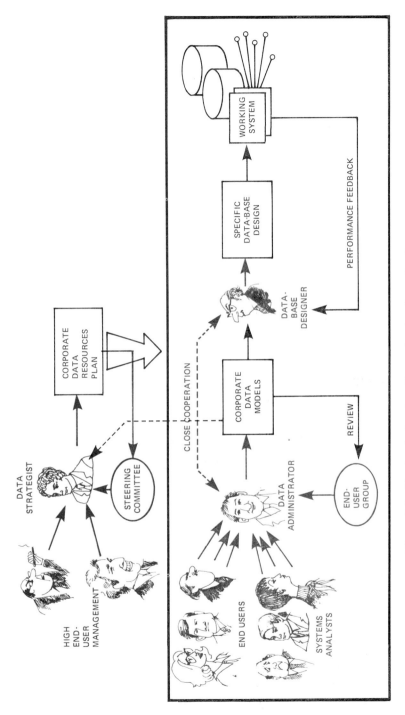

Figure 3.8 Top-level planning directs the data-base development process.

One finds several different ways of dividing up the tasks shown in Fig. 3.8, although the division in Fig. 3.8 may work the best. Particularly important is the end-user involvement illustrated in Fig. 3.8.

POLITICS   The plan in Fig. 3.3 did not work out as shown in practice because it encompassed too many organizations which were politically separate (listed at the top right). The plan used needs to be implementable in practice with the human organizations involved, and needs to have top management commitment to the implementation effort.

Sensitivity to the way separate divisions or suborganizations are managed is needed. In some cases they will remain inevitably separate and the plan should take this into account. In other cases the plan has been needlessly torn apart by end users pulling in opposite directions or opposing the data-base approach. This situation requires strong direction from the top—a suitable mix of user education, top-level directives, and sensitivity to the personalities involved. This is one reason why top management needs to understand and endorse the data-base approach.

If top management is clearly saying "This corporation is going to be run with data bases, and all user managements are expected to help," this directive solves many problems!

A LONG JOURNEY   A corporation setting out to build a comprehensive set of data bases has a long journey ahead of it. However, it has to be done sooner or later.

The early stages of the journey should be individual systems for well-defined purposes. It is generally better to start with **operations systems** for well-specified applications rather than general-purpose **information systems,** and to select those operations systems which appear to offer tangible reward. The information systems may arise, in part, as a by-product of the operations systems.

There is a **major** difference however, between a route which gives the best short-term results irrespective of the final goal and a route which is planned to eventually lead to a comprehensive goal which being profitable, insofar as possible, in the short term.

Different systems and applications in a corporation will necessarily evolve separately because of the high complexity involved and the limited span of the minds of implementors. It is essential to ensure that they **can** evolve separately, implemented by teams with localized knowledge, because only in that way can they be closely tailored to the needs of the persons who will use the systems; only in that way can the high level of initiative and inventiveness of the local implementors be fully utilized. Nevertheless, it is desirable that, insofar as possible, the data-processing designers have a **master plan** for the future evolution of data bases in their organization. Centralized control is necessary to ensure an adequate measure of compatibility between the systems. Without such advanced planning the systems become more difficult (and in many cases have proved virtually impossible) to link together. They incur high costs for program or data conversion. They are often more difficult for the terminal operators to use because different terminal dialogue structures are used for different systems. They are much more cumbersome in the data-base planning, and more expensive in application of resources and in telecommunication costs. The linking together of separately designed and incompatible systems has proved to be extremely expensive in practice. In many cases the magnitude of the programming effort has been comparable to that when the systems were first installed.

Unfortunately, the adherence to a neatly conceived master plan has rarely been achieved in reality. The state of the art is moved by unpredictable tides, and their pressures are strong enough to distort the best-laid plans. A certain machine or software package suddenly becomes available. One approach works and another fails. Natural selection takes over, and we have a process of evolution dominated by the survival of whatever is the most practical.

The master plan, then, must not be too rigid; indeed, **it is absolutely essential to plan for uncertainty.** It must be permissible for different systems to evolve in their own ways. As they evolve they should employ data which have been defined and modeled independently of specific applications. The corporate **logical data models** are the foundation of separate data-base evolution.

4 WHAT ARE DATA?

BUBBLE CHARTS   The users and analysts need a simple way to understand and represent the nature of their data. The bubble charts described in this chapter provide a way of thinking about data and the associations between data items.

They explain the nature of data very simply so that end users can be taught to use them, draw them, and think about their data with them.

As we shall see in Chapter 5, bubble charts drawn by end users can form a vital input to the data-base design process.

DATA ITEMS   The most elemental piece of data is called a **data item.** It is sometimes also called a **field** or a **data element.**

It is the atom of data, in that it cannot be subdivided into smaller data types and retain any meaning to the users of the data. You cannot split the data item called SALARY, for example, into smaller data items which by themselves are meaningful to end users.

We will draw each **type** of data item as an ellipse:

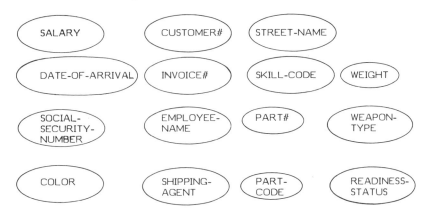

A data base contains hundreds (and sometimes thousands) of types of data items. Five thousand or more types of data items may be used in the running of a big corporation.

In order to computerize the activities of a corporation, the data items it uses must be defined, cataloged, and organized. This is often difficult and time-consuming because data have been treated rather sloppily in the past. What is essentially the same data item has been defined differently in different places, represented differently in computers, and given different names. Data items which were casually thought to be the same are found to be not quite the same. In one insurance company the term POLICY NUMBER was widely used, but as the data bases were being defined it was found that it was used with a dozen different meanings in different places. If a simple term like POLICY NUMBER causes this problem, think of the problem with some of the more subtle terms.

The data administrator has the job of cleaning up this confusion. Definitions of data items must be agreed upon and documented. Much help from end users is often needed in this process.

ASSOCIATIONS
BETWEEN DATA
ITEMS

A data item by itself is not of much use. For example, a value of SALARY by itself is uninteresting. It only becomes interesting when it it associated with another data item, such as EMPLOYEE#. Thus:

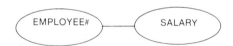

A data base, therefore, consists not only of data items but also of associations between them. There are a large number of different data-item types and we need a map showing how they are associated. This map is sometimes called a **data model.**

SINGLE-HEAD AND
DOUBLE-HEAD
ARROWS

There are two types of links that we shall draw between data items: links with a single-head arrow and links with a double-head arrow.

A single-head arrow from data item A to data item B means that **at each instant in time, each value of A has one and only one value of B associated with it.** There is a one-to-one mapping from A to B. If you know the value of A, then you can know the value of B.

There is only one value of SALARY associated with a value of EMPLOYEE#

at one instant in time; therefore, we can draw a single-head arrow from EMPLOYEE# to SALARY, thus:

It is said that EMPLOYEE# **identifies** SALARY. If you know the value of EMPLOYEE#, then you can know the value of SALARY. The single-head arrow notation is consistent with the notation of mathematical logic in which A → B means A **identifies** B.

A double-head arrow from A to B means that **one value of A has zero, one or many values of B associated with it.** This is a one-to-many mapping from A to B.

While an employee can only have one salary at a given time, he might have zero, one, or many girlfriends. Therefore, we would draw

For one value of the data item EMPLOYEE#, there can be zero, one, or many values of the data item GIRLFRIEND.

We can draw both of the foregoing situations on one bubble chart, thus:

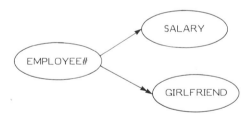

This bubble chart **synthesizes** the two previous charts into one chart. From this one chart we could derive either of the two previous charts.

The two previous charts might be two different user views, one user being interested in salary and the other in girlfriends. We have created one simple data structure which incorporates these two user views. This is what the data administrator does when building a data base, but the real-life user views are much more complicated than the illustration above and there are many of them. The resulting data model sometimes has hundreds or even thousands of data items.

By the way, we need to build privacy controls into a data model. We do not want **any** person who feels like it finding out about our salary and girlfriends! Privacy is discussed in Chapter 9.

MANY OCCURRENCES OF DATA ITEMS The bubble chart shows data-item types. There are many occurrences of each data item. In the example above there are many employees, each with a salary and with zero, one, or many girlfriends. The reader might imagine a third dimension to the bubble charts showing the many values of each data item, thus:

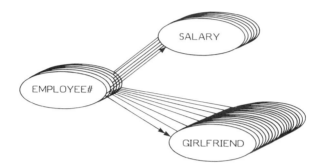

REVERSE ASSOCIATIONS Between any two data items there can be a mapping in both directions. This gives four possibilities for forward and reverse association. If the data-item types are MAN and WOMAN, and the relationship between them represents **marriage,** the four theoretical possibilities are:

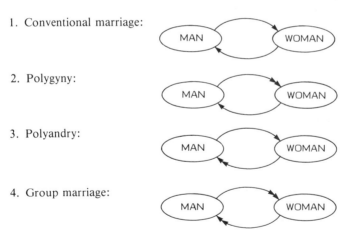

1. Conventional marriage:

2. Polygyny:

3. Polyandry:

4. Group marriage:

The reverse associations are not always of interest. For example, with the data model below we want the reverse association from DEPARTMENT# to EMPLOYEE# because users want to know what employees work in a given department. However, there is no arrow from SPOUSE-NAME to EMPLOYEE# because no user wants to ask "What employee has a spouse named Gertrude?" If a user wanted to ask "What employees have a salary over $25,000?" we would include a double-head arrow from SALARY to EMPLOYEE#.

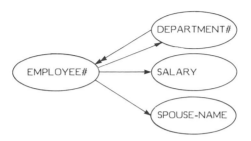

DATA-ITEM GROUPS   Between N data items there are $N(N\text{-}1)$ possible associations. A large data base has more than 1 million **possible** associations between data items. It would be impractical to handle all of them, so the data items are arranged into groups, and we refer to associations between groups. This cuts to a reasonable number the number of associations with which we concern ourselves.

The data-item group is given different names in different data-base management systems—"record," "segment," or "tuple." We will refer to the record, segment, or tuple as a **data-item group.**

We will draw the data-item groups as a bar containing the names of the data items. Thus:

SUPPLIER#	SUPPLIER-NAME	SUPPLIER-ADDRESS	SUPPLIER-DETAILS

This data-item group represents the following bubble chart:

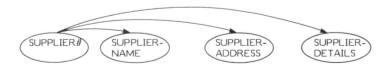

We use single-head arrows and double-head arrows to link the data-item groups. They have the same one-to-one and one-to-many meanings.

Thus, in the following data base there are several suppliers for one part, many outstanding orders for one supplier, several order items on one order, and so on.

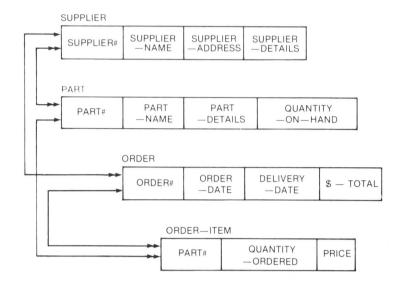

KEYS AND ATTRIBUTES

Given the bubble chart method of representing data, we can state three important definitions.

1. PRIMARY KEY
2. SECONDARY KEY
3. NONPRIME ATTRIBUTE

A primary key is a bubble with one or more single-head arrows leaving it. Thus, in the following diagram A, C, and F are primary keys:

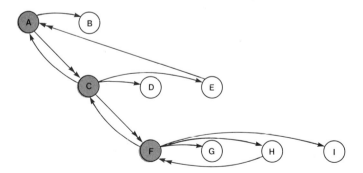

Data items which are not primary keys are referred to as **nonprime attributes.** All data items, then, are either **primary keys** or **nonprime attributes.** In the diagram above, B, D, E, G, H, and I are attributes.

To highlight the distinction, primary keys will be colored red in our diagrams. We can define a nonprime attribute as follows:

A nonprime attribute is a bubble with no single-head arrows leaving it.

Each primary key uniquely identifies one or more data items.

A **secondary key** does not uniquely identify another data item. One value of a secondary key is associated with zero, one, or many values of another data item. In other words, there is a double-head arrow going from it to that other item.

A secondary key is a nonprime attribute with one or more double-head arrows leaving it.

In the diagram above, E and H are secondary keys.

For emphasis the box below repeats these three fundamental definitions.

A **PRIMARY KEY** is a bubble with one or more single-head arrows leaving it.

A **NONPRIME ATTRIBUTE** is a bubble with no single-head arrows leaving it.

A **SECONDARY KEY** is a nonprime attribute with one or more double-head arrows leaving it.

DATA-ITEM GROUPS   In the bubble chart which results from combining many user views, the bubbles are grouped by primary key. Each primary key is the unique identifier of a data-item group. It points with single-head arrows to each nonprime attribute in that data-item group.

The data-item group needs to be structured carefully so that it is as stable as possible. We should not group together an **ad hoc** collection of data items. There are formal rules for structuring the data-item group, which we discuss later.

ENTITIES   We refer to items about which we store information as *entities.* An entity may be real or abstract, tangible or nontangible.

Examples of tangible entities are *a customer, an employee, an invoice, a machine tool, a part, and a department.*

Examples of nontangible entities are *an event, a job title, a time period, a profit center, and an abstract concept.*

An entity has various *attributes* which we wish to record, such as *color, size, monetary value, percentage utilization, address, salary, date, type-code, and sex.*

For each type of entity one type of record is usually kept. The record has a **primary key** which uniquely identifies it, and a variable number of attributes. Similar records are grouped into logical *files.* The result is shown in Fig. 4.1.

Inside the box in Fig. 4.1 is a set of data items. The value of each data item is shown. Each row of data items relates to a particular entity. Each column contains a particular type of data item, relating to a particular type of attribute. At the top of the diagram, outside the box, the names of the attributes are written. The left-most column in the box contains the data items which *identify* the entity. The entity in this example is a person, an employee. The attribute referred to as the entity identifier in this case is EMPLOYEE NUMBER.

Such a two-dimensional array is sometimes referred to as a *flat file.* The use of flat files dates back to the earliest days of data processing when the file might have been on punched cards. Each card in a file or deck of cards such as that in Fig. 4.2 might contain one record, relating to one entity. Certain card columns were allocated to each data-item type, or attribute, and were called a *field.* When magnetic tapes replaced decks of cards and disks replaced magnetic tapes, many programmers retained their view of data as being organized into flat files. No matter how the data are stored in a data base, the software must present the data to the application program in flat-file form if that is the way the program is written.

A medium-sized corporation typically has several hundred entities. Often, however, there are *thousands* of types of records because uncontrolled redundancy has grown up. This redundancy often results in more application programming than is necessary, complex maintenance, difficulty of obtaining summary information for management, and lack of corporate control.

Each *entity* often has ten or more *attributes.* A corporation with several hundred entities has several thousand attributes.

CONCATENATED KEYS   Some data items cannot be identified by any one single data item in a user's view. They need a primary key (unique identifier) which is composed of more than one data item in combination. This is called a concatenated key.

Several suppliers may supply a part and each charge a different price for it. The primary key SUPPLIER# is used for identifying information about a **supplier.** The key PART# is used for identifying information about a **part.** Neither of those keys is sufficient for identifying the **price.** The price is dependent on both the supplier and the part. We create a new key to identify the price, which consists of SUPPLIER# and PART# joined together (concatenated). We draw this as one bubble:

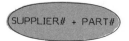

SUPPLIER# + PART#

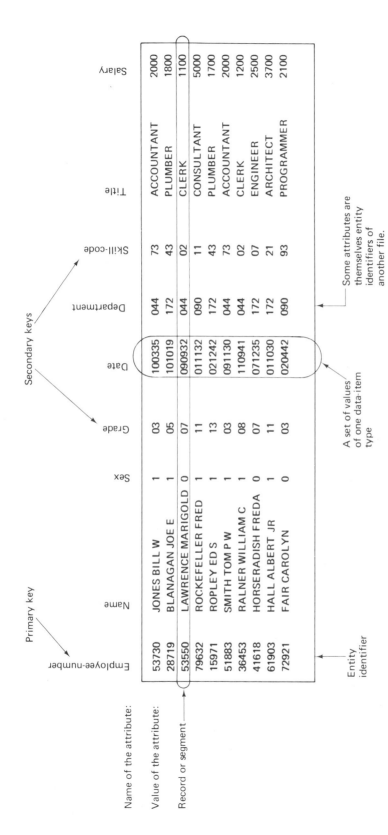

Figure 4.1 The records for the EMPLOYEE entity, which has a primary key: EMPLOYEE-NUMBER.

45

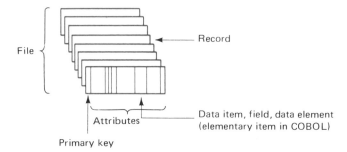

Figure 4.2 A flat file, showing the wording commonly used to describe the application programmer's view of data. Most decks of punched cards are flat files.

The two fields from which the concatenated key is created are joined with a " + " symbol.

The concatenated key has single-arrow links to the keys SUPPLIER# and PART#. The resulting graph is as follows:

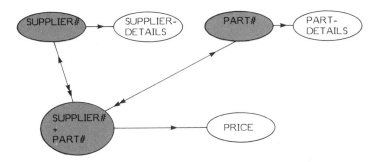

By introducing this form of concatenated key into the logical view of data, we make each nonprime attribute dependent on one key bubble.

Whenever a concatenated key is introduced, the designer should ensure that the items it identifies are dependent on the whole key, not on a portion of it only.

In practice it is sometimes necessary to join together **more than two** data items in a concatenated key.

For example, a company supplies a product to domestic and industrial customers. It charges a different price to different **types of customers,** and also the price varies from one **state** to another. There is a **discount** giving different price reductions for different quantities purchased. The **price** is identified by a combination of CUSTOMER-TYPE, STATE, DISCOUNT, and PRODUCT. Thus:

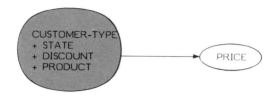

The use of concatenated keys gives each data-item group in the resulting data model a simple structure in which each nonprime attribute is fully dependent on the key bubble and nothing else:

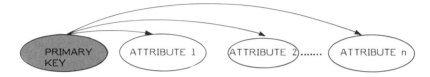

MULTIPLE ASSOCIATIONS BETWEEN DATA ITEMS

On rare occasions it is necessary to have two associations between the same two bubbles. Suppose that we have a data item called PERSON and a data item called DOG, and we want to represent which dogs a person owns and also which dogs a person has been bitten by.

We would draw

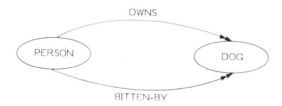

Because there are two links between the same two data items, the links are labeled.

Situations like this requiring labeled associations can usually be avoided by introducing an extra data-item type, thus:

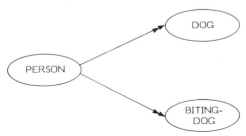

A single-head arrow may go from both of the DOG data items above to PERSON to show who owns what dog. The owner of the biting dogs may then be traced.

In general it is recommended that labeled associations be avoided, where possible.

5 DATA MODELING

LOGICAL DESIGN The single factor most critical to the success of data-base installations is the overall **logical** design of the data base.

A data base contains hundreds (and sometimes thousands) of types of data items. These data-item types have to be associated into a data-base structure. How do you organize them into a logical structure? What is the best logical structure?

This question is vitally important because that logical structure is the foundation stone on which most future data processing will be built. Not only will conventional programs be written to use the data base but, increasingly, higher-level data-base languages will be used which enable users to extract the information they need from the data base directly, and sometimes to update the data bases. The future corporation will be managed with data-base resources, networks to access the data bases, and end-user software for employing and updating the data.

If the logical structures are designed badly, a large financial penalty will result. A corporation will not be able to employ the data bases as it should, so productivity will suffer. The data bases will constantly have to be modified, but they cannot be modified without much application program rewriting. The end users will not be served as they need, and because of this many try to create their own alternatives to employing the data base.

In the late 1970s it became clear that many data-base installations were not living up to the publicized advantages of data base. Why the difference? Time and time again the difference lay in the design of the overall logical structure of the data.

In many data-base installations more than half of the money being spent on application development is being used for rewriting what has already been written. The euphemism "maintenance" is used for this. Maintenance means changing old programs, restructuring data, and subsequently having to rewrite the programs which use that data. One of the arguments for using data-base management systems

49

is that they greatly reduce such maintenance. Why has this not worked in many installations? The answer lies again in the logical structuring of the data.

There are formal techniques for structuring the data in such a way that maintenance costs are minimized (5, 6). They have worked very successfully in installations which have used them. They are concerned with how the data items are grouped into records, segments, and tuples, and how these are linked into data-base structures. Any data-base installation which does not model its data in such a form before doing the physical design is throwing money down the drain. It is condemning itself to large future maintenance costs and inability to respond to many users' needs.

**DATA
ADMINISTRATION**
The task of designing the logical structure of data is done by a **data administrator.** Sometimes the person who designs the logical structure also designs the physical structure. In large organizations, or organizations with complex data, the logical design is done by a different person to the physical design.

The logical designer works with the systems analysts and end users of data to find out what data are needed for their operations. The data items are defined and cataloged in a **data dictionary.** The data structures needed for different users are determined and are synthesized into the data-base structure.

A data base can be defined as a collection of data from which multiple different end-user views are derived.

The task of designing a data base is then to capture the end-user views and synthesize them into a data-base structure (Fig. 5.1).

However, the resulting structure needs to be as stable as possible. If it has to be changed in certain ways in the future it will force the rewriting of application programs. This is expensive, sometimes so expensive in practice that it is never done and so vital data-base uses are postponed.

A key to success in data modeling is for the data administrator to involve the end users as fully as possible.

The users should be asked to think about the data they need for running their function, to participate in defining the data items, and to check the output from the data-modeling process.

It helps greatly if selected end users can draw the data structures they need. To do this, they need to learn the material in Chapter 4 and to practice drawing the bubble charts described. Experience has shown that after minimal training, users are capable of developing the views of data which relate to their job.

A technique which has proved highly successful is to form an end-user committee as discussed in Chapter 3. The committee is composed of selected users who meet periodically with the data administrator will think about the data structures

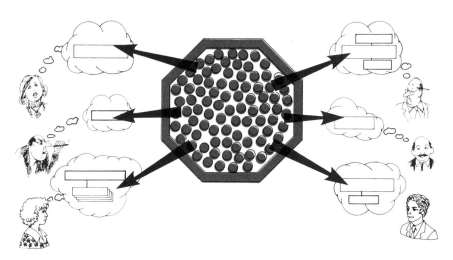

A data base can be defined as a collection of data from which multiple different end-user views are derived.

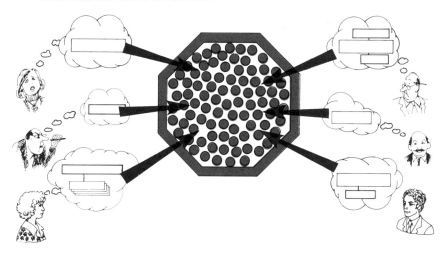

The task of designing the data is then to capture the end-user views and
synthesize them into a data-base structure. The resulting structure must be
as stable as possible and must represent the inherent properties of the data.

Figure 5.1

needed in their area. The data administrator, with the help of systems analysts,
feeds the user views of data into a data-modeling process and at the same time into
a data dictionary. The output of the dictionary and data-modeling process are then
given to the user committee.

Normally, there will be much argument about the definitions of data items
and about which data items are standard. It is the task of the data administrator to

resolve these arguments. The personality of some highly successful data administrators is that of a diplomat rather than that of a technician. An appropriate design tool can make the technical aspects of the job simple and allow the data administrator to concentrate on the most difficult problem: the true nature and definitions of the data. This assumes that a separate person performs the physical implementation (a highly technical job), as in Fig. 3.5.

END-USER ITERATIONS   When the users look at the resulting design, they often suggest changes. It is desirable that these changes be made quickly so that the users can see their effects on the overall design.

If the modeling is done by computer changes can be made quickly. The effects of these changes need not be inserted into the official data model until they have been examined by the systems analysts and users. This fast automated response to suggested changes enables the data-base design process to be highly interactive, which is what it should be. The data administrator can experiment with various forms of user requirements quickly and easily. In particular, he should think about future needs to determine how data models serving future applications fit in with what is being done today. The impact of proposed systems on the existing data base can be evaluated quickly.

When the data administrator has to do **manual** designs this is a slow, tedious, and error-prone process. The result is usually not an optimal structure. Because it is so tedious and time-consuming the data administrator avoids repeatedly redoing the design. But this repeated redesign is often very important in clarifying the nature of the data. **The more thinking, iteration, and interaction with the users that goes on before a data base is implemented, the better the final product will be.**

We discuss these tools in Chapter 6.

CLEAR   Many data-base designers have flip charts on sheets of
REPRESENTATION   paper with arrows straggling wildly out of control from
                       one block to another. Pointers to pointers to pointers.
A bird's nest of linkages, frequently patched, often incomplete, almost impossible for a third party to check. This type of confused diagram leads to bad data-base design and prevents effective communication with the users. A good modeling tool should draw clear diagrams of data-base structures. Changes should be simple to make and when made it should redraw the diagrams. These diagrams can be given to analysts and users to check, think about, and provide feedback for redesigns. Along with the data dictionary, they form the basis for that communication link with user departments without which data-base installations will not be truly successful.

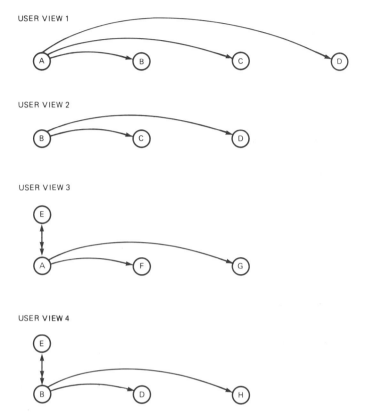

Figure 5.2   Four user views of data.

SYNTHESIS   The data-modeling process takes many separate user
                       views of data and **synthesizes** them into a structure
which incorporates all of them, as illustrated in Fig. 5.1.

The synthesis is done in such a way that redundant data items are eliminated
where possible. The same data item does not generally appear twice in the final
result. Also, redundant **associations** are eliminated where possible. In other words,
a minimal number of lines connects the bubbles in the resulting bubble chart.

The synthesis process is a formal procedure following a formal set of rules.
Because it is a formal procedure it can be done by a computer. This eliminates errors in the process, provides formal documentation which is a basis for end-user
discussion, and permits any input view to be changed or new views to be added and
immediately reflects the effect of the change in the resulting data model.

There is **only one** data model which is a minimal nonredundant synthesis of
any given collection of user bubble charts.

SYNTHESIS   As a simple illustration of the synthesis process, con-
ILLUSTRATION   sider the four user views of data shown in Fig. 5.2. We
                       want to combine those into a single data model.

To start, here is view 1:

We will combine view 2 with it: Here's view 2.

Here is the combination of views 1 and 2.
None of the data items above appear twice in the result:

There are, however, some redundant links.

- A identifies B.

- And B identifies C.

- Therefore, A **must** identify C.

- Therefore, the link A → C is redundant.

- Similarly, A identifies B and B identifies D; therefore, A **must** identify D. Therefore, the link A → D is redundant.

The redundant links are removed and we have

Now the third view:

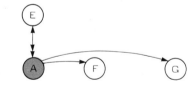

This contains three data items, E, F, and G. When it is merged into the model, we get

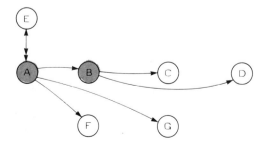

There are no new redundancies, so we will merge in the fourth view:

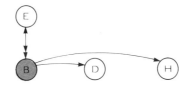

This adds one new data item to the model, H:

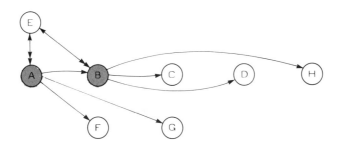

There is now one redundant link.

A identifies B; B identifies E; therefore, **A must** identify E. We can remove the single-head arrow from A to E (we cannot change the double-head arrow from E to A):

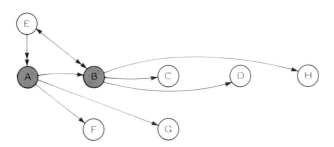

In this resulting structure there are two primary keys: A and B. (A primary key is a bubble with one or more single-head arrows leaving it.)

We can associate each primary key with the attributes it identifies:

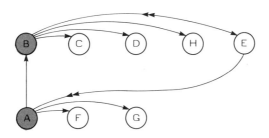

On each linkage between primary keys it is desirable to put the reverse link-age. We should therefore ask: Is the link from B to A a double-head arrow or single-head arrow link?

Suppose that it is a double-head arrow link. The following diagram draws the logical data-item groups (records, segments, tuples) that result from this design:

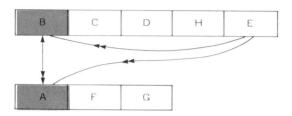

Here, E is a secondary key pointing to both A and B. In old punched-card or batch-processing systems, secondary keys, such as E, were the **sort** keys. In on-line systems, secondary key paths such as those from E to A or B are followed by such means as pointers or indices.

Reference 6 gives more details of this data-modeling process, with more com-plex examples. Appendix 1 of the present book lists a manual procedure for the modeling process.

6 DESIGN TOOLS FOR END USERS

INTRODUCTION   Data-base designers use a variety of design tools. Two of them are important to the end users: the data dictionary and the logical modeling tool. Both have input which comes from an understanding of the users' data needs and definitions. Both create output which becomes formal documentation of the data and which should be reviewed by the end users to make sure that it represents their needs correctly.

There are many data dictionaries on the market. Data-modeling tools are less common. Both should be regarded as important for success in data-base installations.

DATA DICTIONARY   A data dictionary is a tool which lists all data items that are used, their definitions, how and where they are used, and who is responsible for them. In a distributed environment the dictionary ought to be accessible via terminals so that the same definitions are available to all locations.

Figure 6.1 shows sample entries in a data dictionary used in a personnel example. Data items such as those in Fig. 6.1 are employed by different types of users for different purposes. There is sometimes considerable debate at the data-base user group meetings before common definitions are agreed upon.

When data at geographically dispersed sites are used via a communications network, the fields at all locations should be in the dictionary. It is desirable that the same dictionary be used for an entire corporation or corporate subsidiary or division.

The dictionary helps to enforce agreement on the definition of each data item and its bit structure. It helps to avoid having different data items with the same name (homonyms) and the same data items having different names in different places (synonyms). In some cases the same data item does have different names for historical reasons, and the dictionary informs its users of these aliases. The dictionary is a vital tool for enabling different users to agree about the definitions of the data needed to run a computerized corporation.

The dictionary says how data items are arranged into the records, segments, or tuples of a data base. It may indicate where data reside geographically, and what data are replicated at different locations. It indicates which programs read the data, and which update them. It should indicate who is responsible for the accuracy of the data, who update them, and who can read them.

The dictionary user can request a variety of reports from it. A designer at one location can ask to see where else his data are used. A data administrator faced with

---

DATABASE　　　　HUMAN-RESOURCE

THE HUMAN RESOURCE DATA BASE CONTAINS THE INFORMATION RELATED TO PERSONNEL, PAYROLL, SKILLS, AND BENEFITS. IT IS MAINTAINED BY THE VARIOUS SUBSYSTEMS THAT MAKE UP THE HUMAN RESOURCES APPLICATION SYSTEM. IT IS USED FOR REPORTING BY THESE SAME SUBSYSTEMS AS WELL AS THE MANAGEMENT REPORTING SYSTEM AND ACCOUNTING REPORTING SYSTEM.

AREA　　　　PAYROLL

THE PAYROLL AREA CONSISTS OF THE PAYROLL MASTER FILE AND CONTAINS INFORMATION REGARDING ALL PAY-UNITS. IT IS MANAGED BY THE PAYROLL DEPARTMENT.

FILE　　　　PAYROLL-MASTER

THE PAYROLL MASTER FILE CONTAINS A RECORD FOR EACH EMPLOYEE IN-CLUDING ACTIVE EMPLOYEES, TERMINATED EMPLOYEES, AND SUSPENSIONS.

RECORD　　　　PAYROLL

THE PAYROLL RECORD CONTAINS EMPLOYEES NUMBER HIS/HERS PAY CODE AND RATE OF PAY WHICH ALSO INCLUDES TAX INFORMATION.

KEY　　　　PAYROLL NUMBER

THE EMPLOYEE NUMBER KEY IS USED TO RANDOMLY ACCESS PAYROLL RECORDS FOR IDENTIFICATION AND TAX REPORTING PURPOSES. ONCE ENTERED, AN EMPLOYEE NUMBER SHOULD NOT BE MODIFIED.

FIELD　　　　PAYROLL ACTIVITY-CODE

THE EMPLOYEE ACTIVITY-CODE ELEMENT CONTAINS THE EMPLOYEE NUMBER AND EMPLOYEE PAY CODE AND STATUS CODE.

FIELD　　　　PAYROLL EMPLOYEE-CODE

EMPLOYEE CODE IS ONE CHARACTER FIELD THAT CONTAINS THE EMPLOYEES PAY TYPE. IT SHOULD CONTAIN —H— FOR HOURLY OR —S— SALARY. THIS IS USED FOR PAY RATE AND YEAR TO DATE INFORMATION.

Figure 6.1　A verbal description of the use of fields, keys, records, data bases, etc. This illustration is from ADR's dictionary for their DATACOM relational data base.

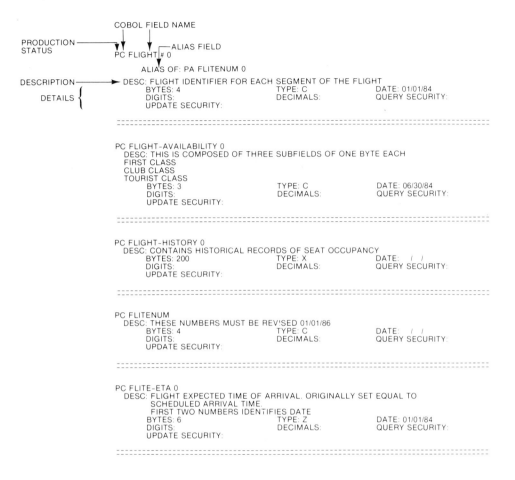

Figure 6.2 The user of the IBM DB/DC data dictionary requests a list of all data items (elements) with production status, where the subject code is COBOL, and the data item name includes the character string 'FLI':

the prospect of changing a certain data item can ask what programs use that data item. Figure 6.2 and 6.3 show some typical data dictionary reports. A programmer or analyst starts off with well-documented data.

　　Some dictionaries automatically generate the program language descriptions of data that programmers use. They will generate the control blocks and parameters required by data-base management systems. This automatic generation of data for programs ensures that the programmer cannot ignore data definition standards. It helps the programmer avoid inaccuracies. It also saves him time in coding (enough time to pay for itself, usually) and it does part of the program documentation in a formal fashion.

```
LIST OF SELECTED MEMBERS
MEMBER NAME                          TYPE       USAGE  CONDITION   AC   ALT  REM  OWNER

EMPLOYEE-CODE                        ITEM         7    SCE  ENC   YES  YES  YES  PERSONNEL
EMPLOYEE-DATE                        ITEM         1     ·   DUM   YES  YES  YES
EMPLOYEE-HISTORY-RECORD              GROUP        1    SCE  ENC   YES  YES  YES
EMPLOYEE-HISTORY-REPORT              FILE         2    SCE  ENC   YES  YES  YES
EMPLOYEE-MASTER-RECORD               GROUP        1    SCE  ENC   YES  YES  YES
EMPLOYEE-REPORT                      FILE         2    SCE  ENC   YES  YES  YES
EMPLOYEE-REPORT-HEADER               GROUP        3    SCE  ENC   YES  YES  YES
EMPLOYEE-REPORT-RECORD               GROUP        1    SCE  ENC   YES  YES  YES
EMPLOYEE-TRANSACTIONS-FORM           GROUP        2    SCE  ENC   YES  YES  YES
PM1                                  ITEM         2     ·   DUM   YES  YES  YES
PM2                                  ITEM         2     ·   DUM   YES  YES  YES
PM3                                  ITEM         2     ·   DUM   YES  YES  YES
PM4                                  ITEM         2     ·   DUM   YES  YES  YES
PM5                                  ITEM         1     ·   DUM   YES  YES  YES
P1-ERS                               SYSTEM       0    SCE  ENC   YES  YES  YES
P1I01                                MODULE       2    SCE  ENC   YES  YES  YES
P1P01                                PROGRAM      1    SCE  ENC   YES  YES  YES
P1S01                                PROGRAM      1    SCE  ENC   YES  YES  YES
P1S01TSORT                           FILE         3    SCE  ENC   YES  YES  YES
P1U01                                PROGRAM      1    SCE  ENC   YES  YES  YES
P1U02                                MODULE       1    SCE  ENC   YES  YES  YES
P1U02MEMP                            FILE         5    SCE  ENC   YES  YES  YES
P1V01                                PROGRAM      1    SCE  ENC   YES  YES  YES
P1V01WVAL                            FILE         2    SCE  ENC   YES  YES  YES
P2-EHS                               SYSTEM       0    SCE  ENC   YES  YES  YES
P2P01                                PROGRAM      1    SCE  ENC   YES  YES  YES
P2U01                                PROGRAM      1    SCE  ENC   YES  YES  YES
P2U01TEMP                            FILE         3    SCE  ENC   YES  YES  YES
REPORT-PAGE                          ITEM         1    SCE  ENC   YES  YES  YES
REPORT-TITLE                         ITEM         1    SCE  ENC   YES  YES  YES
STANDARD-DATE                        ITEM         4    SCE  ENC   YES  YES  YES
TRANSACTION-CODE                     ITEM         4    SCE  ENC   YES  YES  YES
TRANSACTION-RECORD                   GROUP        4    SCE  ENC   YES  YES  YES
UPDATE-CONTROL-RECORD                GROUP        1    SCE  ENC   YES  YES  YES
UPDATE-CONTROL-REPORT                FILE         2    SCE  ENC   YES  YES  YES

LIST CONTAINS        11 ITEMS
                      7 GROUPS
                      7 FILES
                      2 MODULES
                      6 PROGRAMS
                      2 SYSTEMS
                      6 DUMMIES
                     35 MEMBERS IN TOTAL
```

The user asks which files and programs use the data-item DEPARTMENT:

```
                    WHICH FILES USE DEPARTMENT.

THE FOLLOWING USE ITEM DEPARTMENT
     FILES             EMPLOYEE-MASTER
                       EMPLOYEE-HISTORY-MASTER
                       EMPLOYEE-HISTORY-LIST
                       EMPLOYEE-LIST
                       EMPLOYEE-TRANSACTIONS
                       EMPLOYEE-TRANSACTIONS-SORTED


                    WHICH PROGRAMS USE DEPARTMENT.

THE FOLLOWING USE ITEM DEPARTMENT
     PROGRAMS          CALCULATE-GROSS-EARNINGS
                       EMPLOYEE-HISTORY-REPORT
                       EMPLOYEE-MASTER-UPDATE
                       EMPLOYEE-REPORT
                       EMPLOYEE-HISTORY-UPDATE
                       EMPLOYEE-VET
```

Figure 6.3 (courtesy MSP) The user of the MSP data dictionary requests a list of data items, groups, files or any other components of the data base which are new or changed.

DATA-MODELING TOOL   The data-modeling tool does the data synthesis which we described in Chapter 5. It does it in a formal fashion. The words "third normal form" and "canonical synthesis" are used to describe formally designed stable data structures (5, 6). The modeling tool should create data in this form. This is a simple, clean, structure of data, intended to help the data administrator make the data base as stable as possible, thereby avoiding large future maintenance and conversion costs.

The bubble charts showing data, which the systems analyst or end user draws, can be fed into the tool one at a time. The tool synthesizes them into the model structure. It draws the resulting structure and produces various reports.

The output of the modeling process should be studied by concerned users, together with dictionary output, to ensure that the data bases being designed do indeed meet their needs.

The data model created by the tool serves as a basis for the task of physical data-base design. The synthesis process can show the frequency of usage of the various usage paths through the data base. This enables the designer to make decisions about how the data should be grouped into the structures (CODASYL sets, DL/I physical data bases, pointers, etc.) that the data-base management system employs.

Figure 6.4 at the end of this book shows a plot of a data model created by DATA DESIGNER. The data items in it are defined in a dictionary output like that in Fig. 6.1. As new views of data are fed into DATA DESIGNER, it adjusts the model as needed.

The data model description and the data dictionary listings together form a fundamental representation of the data needed to run an organization. As the networks and data bases used in running an organization build up, so the data which they employ **or will employ in the future** should be thought about and represented in this formal way.

In most corporations the data are in somewhat of a mess. Different computers have been used without coordinating their data structures. Different files have been created by different programmers and analysts. To successfully build a computerized corporation with data bases and networks, sooner or later the data have to be cleaned up. The same data-item type has to be represented in the same way in different files, different applications, and different machines. Definitions of data items have to be agreed upon. The data items should be structured into cleanly thought out data models.

APPLICATION   When an application is needed, there is usually a high
PRESSURE   level of pressure to complete it quickly. Over and over
again one observes the application pressure being so great that there is no time to complete the data-modeling and definition process. Usually, this process takes much longer than expected.

The modeling tools help to speed up the process and to formalize it to ensure that it is done well.

Even **with** such tools the application pressure is often too great. Corners are cut. Data bases are implemented for urgent applications, ignoring all other applications of the same data. This will ultimately cause high maintenance costs. Sooner or later the data will have to be cleaned up and converted, and that will mean expensive reprogramming.

What is the answer? The answer is to **keep ahead** with the modeling process. Defining and cleaning up the data needed in an organization should be an ongoing activity independent of current application pressures. When those pressures arise, if the data have already been designed, the implementation can proceed more quickly. In fact, if data bases already exist containing that data, this should substantially speed up the implementation, especially if higher-level data-base languages can be used.

Data definition and modeling is a fundamental process essential to building a computerized corporation. It should proceed independently, and throughout the entire organization the same dictionary should be used.

CODING THE BUBBLE CHARTS

To present a user view of data to the data modeling tool, that view must be encoded. This can be a simple process. The bubble charts of Chapter 4 can be translated directly into code and keyed into a terminal.

When DATA DESIGNER is used, each entry normally refers to one data item on a bubble chart (6). Each entry consists of a code character and comma followed by a name, thus:

> K, EMPLOYEE#
> 1, EMPLOYEE-NAME
> 1, AGE

The code character (K and 1 above) is called a **modeling command.**

Code K is used for indicating the data item at **the start of a bubble-chart arrow.** (K stands for **Key.**)

The data item at the other end of the arrow is indicated with a code 1 if it is **one-to-one** association (a single-head arrow), and a code M if it is a **one-to-many** association (a double-head arrow).

Thus

is coded

> K, EMPLOYEE#
> 1, EMPLOYEE-NAME
> 1, AGE

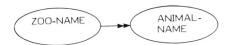

is coded

> K, ZOO-NAME
> M, ANIMAL-NAME

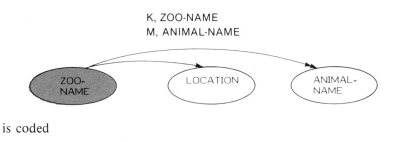

is coded

> K, ZOO-NAME
> 1, LOCATION
> M, ANIMAL-NAME

The data item labeled K can have a list of data items associated with it without its name being repeated. The list may not contain another K data item.

To code two arrows in a string, two K data items are used, thus:

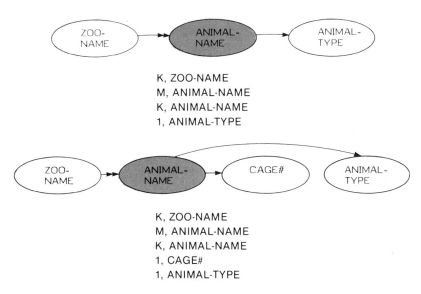

> K, ZOO-NAME
> M, ANIMAL-NAME
> K, ANIMAL-NAME
> 1, ANIMAL-TYPE

> K, ZOO-NAME
> M, ANIMAL-NAME
> K, ANIMAL-NAME
> 1, CAGE#
> 1, ANIMAL-TYPE

To lessen the amount of typing, a name which is the same as in the previous entry need not be repeated, thus:

K, ZOO-NAME
M, ANIMAL-NAME
K
1, ANIMAL-TYPE

A concatenated field is represented with one of the data-item entries above, followed by one or more data items with a C code (C for Concatenated), thus:

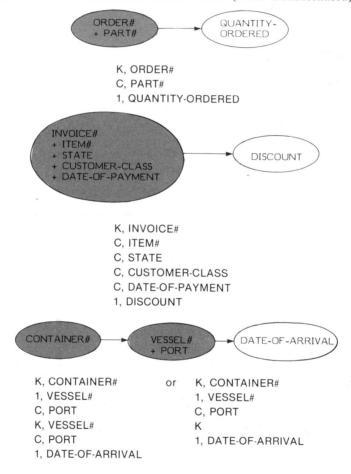

K, ORDER#
C, PART#
1, QUANTITY-ORDERED

K, INVOICE#
C, ITEM#
C, STATE
C, CUSTOMER-CLASS
C, DATE-OF-PAYMENT
1, DISCOUNT

K, CONTAINER#   or   K, CONTAINER#
1, VESSEL#   1, VESSEL#
C, PORT   C, PORT
K, VESSEL#   K
C, PORT   1, DATE-OF-ARRIVAL
1, DATE-OF-ARRIVAL

On the right in the example above, the blank K field picks up the value of the entire concatenated field (the entire bubble), not just part of it.

Using this simple form of coding, one user view after another can be fed to the data modeling tool. It synthesizes them into a structure designed to be stable [a canonical, third-normal-form structure (7, 8)]. It permits reports and draws diagrams such as that in Fig. 6.4 describing the resulting model.

The user group should inspect the documentation of the model and ask certain important questions about it which are described in Chapter 7.

7 HOW TO SUCCEED WITH DATA MODELING

STABILITY   The objective of data modeling is to create data bases which are as stable as possible, and from which diverse end users can automatically derive information they need.

The data-base structures will change in the future, but an objective of their design should be to **minimize those types of change that will cause existing application programs to be rewritten.** As we have stressed, it is expensive to rewrite programs—often so expensive that it is avoided or postponed. Often, the developers create separate files or data bases to avoid restructuring an existing system. This results in inflexibilities and makes future maintenance costs higher.

THINKING ABOUT   When the output from the modeling process is re-
THE FUTURE   viewed, this is the time to think about the future. If future requirements can be understood at this stage a better logical design will result with a lower probability of expensive maintenance later.

The users, systems analysts, and data administrator should examine the output and ask themselves "How might these data be used in the future?" Any potential future use should be incorporated provisionally in the model to see whether that use causes changes in the structure of the data-item groups.

Sometimes end users are better at thinking about the future than DP professionals because they know their possible applications better. This is not always the case. Sometimes imaginative systems analysts, or a data administrator, are best at thinking up future uses for the data.

Often, the best way to do it is with a user group meeting, with the users, analysts, and data administrator all trying to brainstorm future uses for the data.

With some data-base management systems, more attributes can be added to an existing data-item group without forcing the rewriting of old programs which use
that group. This is true only if the primary key is not changed. It might be desirable
to leave space in the record in the physical implementation to permit the inclusion
of additional attributes later.

HIDDEN KEYS   What forces program rewriting is a change in the basic
structure of a record. The most common cause of this is
that a data item which is an attribute in the record now becomes a primary key
later. It is easy to spot any such data items in the output of a data modeling tool.
The data administrator, systems analysts, and user committee should examine each
attribute data item in turn and ask *"Could this possibly be used as a primary key in
the future?"* If data items are found which are potential future primary keys, the
decision should be made whether to make them primary keys **now** by giving the
modeling tool new input views. If they are made into primary keys now, this will
possibly save future redesign with extensive program rewriting.

Figure 7.1 illustrates this. It shows a highly simplified model of data for a
shipping company.

We can take each data item which is not by itself a primary key and *ask
whether it could be used as a primary key in the future:*

> VESSEL-NAME: This is equivalent to VESSEL#. VESSEL# is
> used to identify vessels and so there would
> never be **a separate record** with VESSEL-
> NAME as its primary key.

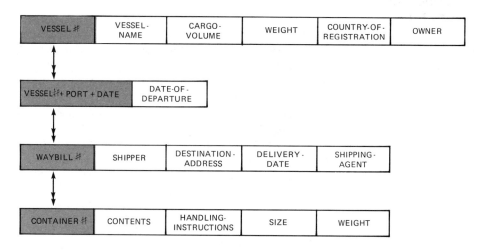

Figure 7.1 Data model for a shipping company.

CARGO-VOLUME:	No. This would not be used as a primary key at any time. (It could conceivably be used as a secondary key. That does not matter.)
WEIGHT:	No.
COUNTRY-OF-REGISTRATION:	No.
OWNER:	Possibly. This deserves discussion. Would future applications use data about the vessel owner?
PORT:	Possibly.
DATE:	No.
DATE-OF-DEPARTURE:	No (though it is likely to be used as a secondary key).
SHIPPER:	Probably. Information not shown in Fig. 7.1 is likely to be stored about the shipper. Another record should therefore be introduced at this stage with a primary key: SHIPPER. There should be discussion about what information about the shipper might be stored.
DESTINATION-ADDRESS:	No.
DELIVERY-DATE:	No.
SHIPPING-AGENT:	Possibly. This should be discussed.
CONTENTS:	No.
HANDLING-INSTRUCTIONS:	No.
SIZE:	No.
WEIGHT:	No.

The data administrator, systems analysts, and end-user group should examine each data item in this way. It is generally easy to spot those which might become primary keys in the future. If they are made primary keys now, that will prevent having to restructure that data and rewrite the programs using it in the future. It could save much money and disruption.

The modeling process will automatically take care of this if views of data using the key in question are fed to it.

DICTIONARY CHECK   When the checks listed above are taking place, the dictionary definitions of the data items should be used in conjunction with the model. Users should double-check that they really represent the true meaning of the data as they are employed by the users.

CAUTION WITH CONCATENATED KEYS

The foregoing items relate to the **output** from the modeling process. Certain cautions are necessary in creating **input** to the process.

First, caution is needed with concatenated keys.

There is a big difference between

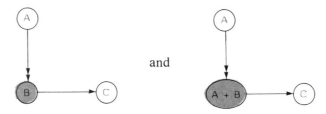

and

It would be incorrect to draw the following:

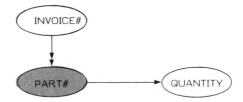

If you know the value of PART#, then you do not know the value of QUANTITY. PART# alone does not identify QUANTITY. To know the value of QUANTITY, you need to know both INVOICE# and PART#. QUANTITY therefore needs to be pointed to by a concatenated key INVOICE# + PART#. The following is correct:

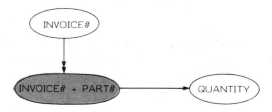

On the other hand,

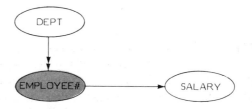

is correct, because EMPLOYEE# *does* (by itself) identify SALARY.

Compare the coding for the two examples above:

```
K, INVOICE#        K, DEPT
M, INVOICE#        M, EMPLOYEE#
C, PART#           K
K                  1, SALARY
1, QUANTITY
```

REVERSE MAPPING
BETWEEN KEYS

DATA DESIGNER, or the modeling process in Appendix 1, wants to know the reverse mapping on any links **between primary keys.** If the user does not enter this, DATA DESIGNER will ask for it. It will be faster for the user to always enter it on any input view.

For example, in the following case:

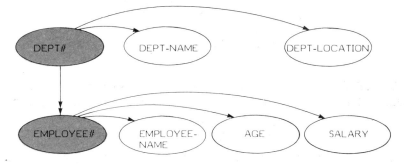

DEPT# and EMPLOYEE# are primary keys. The reverse mapping between them should be entered:

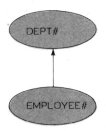

DEPENDENCE ON THE
WHOLE KEY

When attributes are drawn, the user should make sure that they are identified correctly by the primary key which points to them (as above) but also that they are dependent on the **whole** of a concatenated key. Thus, the following is not correct:

PART-DESCRIPTION is identified by only a portion of the concatenated key: PART#. Therefore, a separate key PART# should be drawn:

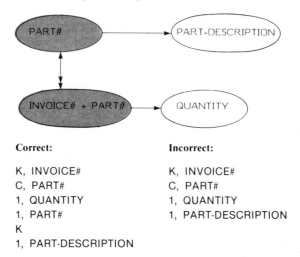

Correct:

K, INVOICE#
C, PART#
1, QUANTITY
1, PART#
K
1, PART-DESCRIPTION

Incorrect:

K, INVOICE#
C, PART#
1, QUANTITY
1, PART-DESCRIPTION

AVOIDANCE OF HIDDEN PRIMARY KEYS

When a data-item group is entered, there may be a hidden primary key in the group. One item entered as an attribute may in fact identify some other data item in the group.

ORDER#	DATE	SUPPLIER#	SUPPLIER-NAME	SUPPLIER-ADDRESS	DELIVERY-DATE	TOTAL

There is a hidden primary key in this record. SUPPLIER# identifies SUPPLIER-NAME and SUPPLIER-ADDRESS. It is therefore not sufficient to draw

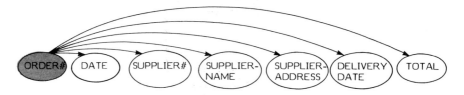

The links from SUPPLIER# to SUPPLIER-NAME and SUPPLIER-ADDRESS should also be drawn:

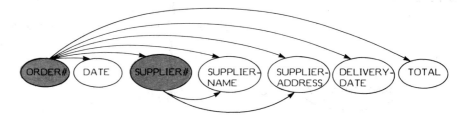

These two extra links make the links

ORDER# ⟶ SUPPLIER-NAME
ORDER# ⟶ SUPPLIER-ADDRESS

redundant. The modeling process will automatically remove them, so the creator of the input need not worry about this.

In brief: **watch out for hidden primary keys!**

CONCATENATED KEYS   When the modeling process in Appendix I, or the modeling tool DATA DESIGNER, encounters a concatenated primary key, it automatically forms the component fields of that key into separate data items. Thus,

becomes

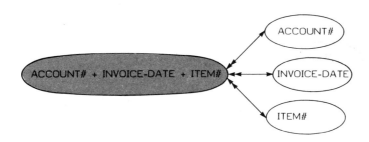

In the example above, ACCOUNT# and ITEM# are keys in their own right. INVOICE-DATE is not. INVOICE-DATE may possibly be deleted, as it is not used as a separate data item.

HOW LARGE SHOULD   When preparing data for the synthesis process, users
USER VIEWS BE?   and analysts have sometimes worried about how complex one user view should be. They have sometimes had difficulty deciding where one user view starts and where it ends.

The answer is: it doesn't matter.

The modeling process combines them into a synthesized structure. A complex user view can be entered as multiple separate user views and the end result will be the same. It is often a good idea to do this because it lessens the likelihood of making an error.

For example, the following bubble chart represents the data on the bills which I receive from a nearby hardware store:

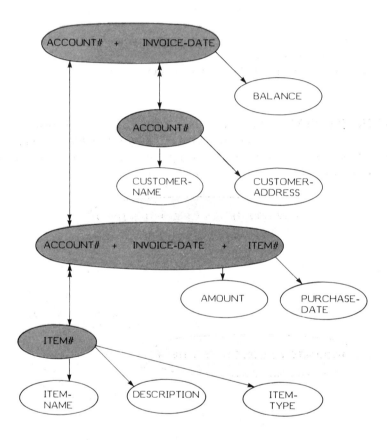

This could be entered in three separate pieces, as follows:

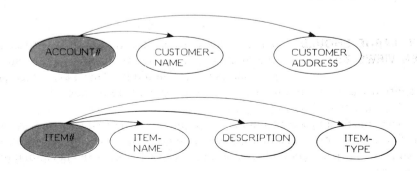

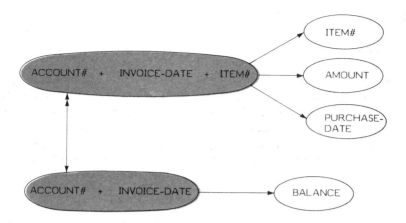

In both cases, ACCOUNT# + INVOICE-DATE + ITEM# would be automatically linked to its component data items: ACCOUNT#, INVOICE-DATE, and ITEM#.

ACCOUNT# + INVOICE-DATE would similarly be linked to ACCOUNT# and INVOICE-DATE. The resulting model would be the same in each case. INVOICE-DATE would not appear as a primary key and hence could be deleted.

CONVERSION AND COMPATIBILITY   Organizations implementing data-base systems usually have old **file** systems, and sometimes old data-base systems which are not in the current form. Sometimes the old data-base systems were badly designed without using the principles which we now understand.

A decision has to be made. Should these old systems be **converted** and their data put in the new data-base form, or should they be allowed to continue to exist? If they are left untouched, some form of bridge will have to be built between the old systems and the new.

Conversion is expensive because if the data are converted, the application programs which use it have to be rewritten. There are often many of these programs—often too many for conversion to be practical or economical.

It is then necessary to build a bridge between these old systems and the new data bases. Transactions or records will pass between the two. These transactions or records should be planned. They will often have the old record format. To ensure compatibility they should be included in the data modeling input views.

The planning of compatibility with past systems is important at the modeling stage. Sometimes designers make the assumption that the past systems will be converted to new ones, but this does not happen because of cost and programmer requirements.

DISTRIBUTED DATA Distributed files or distributed data bases are often used. Files residing on peripheral machines should often be designed to be derivable from a central data-base system. In this case they need to be incorporated as user views in the data modeling process.

Multiple distributed data bases may be derived from a common model.

The great problem of distributed processing is the incompatibility of data on different systems separately implemented. The data modeling output and an associated data dictionary listing provide vital tools for gaining control of the distributed environment. The data-item groups used at multiple locations should be incorporated into a common data dictionary and common set of data models. These should be used for enforcing data standards among the separate locations.

**A SMALL STEP
AT A TIME** The data modeling in an organization needs to be broad in its scope, encompassing the old files and data bases as well as future uses of data. It needs to encompass the many locations where the data will be used. To be successful it usually needs close interaction with end users of many different types.

It should not be regarded as a single task done at one time. It is often too complex for that. Rather, it should be an ongoing process done a small step at a time. The organization's data are steadily cleaned up, removing and documenting the many inconsistencies. A large and complex organization will have multiple different models for different areas. It is easier to do in a small, young, organization that is growing up with computers and possibly minicomputer data-base systems.

The ongoing process of cleaning up, modeling, and documenting the data is an essential part of building a computerized corporation.

8 DATA-BASE LANGUAGES FOR END USERS

One data-base feature is growing in importance so rapidly that it may become the tail which wags the whole dog. It is highly desirable that users who cannot program should be able to query the data bases, extract from them the information they need, generate reports, and in some cases update the data.

For this purpose a wide variety of data-base query languages exist. Some are simple so that an unskilled user such as a clerk can compose a query. Some require more skill and training in order to use them.

Most query languages are advertised as being designed for end users with no programming skill. In spite of what the sales blurb says, some require extensive learning of program-like mnemonics and syntax, and are unlikely to be employed by a manager who approaches a terminal only occasionally. Others are genuinely usable by unskilled users too busy to remember mnemonics and formats.

In order for a data-base query language to be generally employable by a wide cross section of end users, it should follow the rules listed in Box 8.1. It is difficult and unnatural for busy persons to remember codes, formats, and sequences of entry. It should be understood that **powerful** data-base languages can be created which do not force a user to remember such things.

Nevertheless, many data-base languages look as though they were written by programmers for programmers.

INTERACTIVE?
ON-LINE?

Most query languages are designed for interactive use at terminals. Some are designed essentially for off-line use.

With off-line use the user fills in forms or composes queries which are submitted to a computer center. A reply may be received in a few hours, or the following day. An advantage of off-line use is that it places less strain on machine perfor-

75

BOX 8.1

Rules for preprogrammed end-user dialogues

- The means of establishing contact with the computer and signing on should be simple, natural, and **obvious** (with appropriate security routines).

- The user should be required to know as little as possible in order to get started.

- The dialogue should completely avoid forcing the user to remember mnemonics.

- The dialogue should completely avoid forcing the user to remember formats or entry sequences.

- The dialogue should never put the user in a situation where he does not know what to do next.

- The dialogue should provide a simple, natural, and **obvious** means for the user to recover from any mistakes or surprises.

- The response times should be fast enough to avoid frustrating the user.

mance than giving quick answers to a terminal user. Off-line data-base interrogation can be very valuable. One corporation with an IBM data base (using IMS) introduced the capability to interrogate that data base (using GIS, described below) as a supplementary off-line facility. To the amazement of the data-base owners, the users of the data base generated 28,000 reports using the interrogation language in one year of operation. Nevertheless, on-line use can be far more effective than off-line use when the user has the capability to carry on a dialogue with the system. The system can help him to specify complex queries, and he can narrow down his search step by step until he finds the information he is looking for.

It is often the case that the answer to a single off-line query does not provide the information that was sought. The user needs to try a new query or adjust the previous one. Often an initial query is too broad and would result in hundreds of responses or an entire file search. Interactive operation allows the query to be modified so that it is more reasonable before the full search is executed. On some systems the user may adjust his query twenty or thirty times before he finds the information he wants. This depends upon the nature of the query and the nature of the data bases.

SPONTANEITY   Executives who understand that data-base information is available to them sometimes develop many spontaneous ideas for using it. To put the data base to good use for decision making, however, they usually need to receive the information **quickly**—tomorrow they will have a different problem.

As Fig. 8.1 indicates, a vice-president may have to wait weeks or months if a

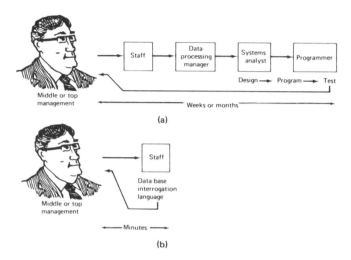

Figure 8.1 An executive can evaluate spontaneous ideas if he receives sufficiently fast responses to his requests for information: (*a*) Using a conventional programming language; (*b*) using a data-base interrogation language.

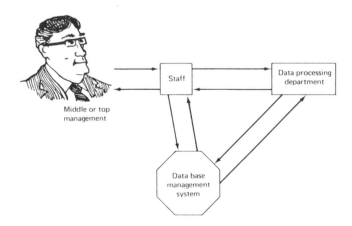

Figure 8.2 The fact that the management staff can interrogate the data base directly takes a load off the data-processing department.

program written in a conventional language is needed to process his information request. With a data-base interrogation language usable by the information staff at terminals, he may receive the information he wants in minutes. Spontaneous ideas involving information usage are encouraged.

As indicated in Fig. 8.2, the fact that the data base can be interrogated directly by the information staff takes a load off the data-processing department.

CAPABILITIES   Typically, capabilities of a powerful data-base language are the following:

- Access to data from remote terminals.
- The ability to let some users read data (only), whereas others can read and update records and possibly insert new records and delete records.
- Report formatting capabilities.
- Computational ability, including addition, subtraction, multiplication, and division.
- Data manipulation capabilities, such as sorting, counting, or totaling items.
- The ability to resequence data and save it for future use.
- The ability to create user files for future use.

DISTRIBUTED FILES   With distributed processing an attractive feature is the ability to create files for end users in a peripheral machine so that users can manipulate or search them without affecting the central data-base or the work load on the central machine. Such features may then reside in the peripheral machine, whereas the data base itself does not.

There is often concern that end users employing a data-base language will harm the integrity of a data base if they are allowed to modify data, and, even if not, may cause performance problems which will interfere with other processing. The performance problems may be especially severe if the users have a language which triggers **secondary key** operations or searches. Because of these concerns it is often good design to place the users' data manipulation activities and information systems in a peripheral computer with separate files. This separate computer handles the data manipulation language (Fig. 8.3). In some cases the peripheral computer is a small minicomputer with good data manipulation capabilities, for example the Microdata **Reality** system.

MULTIPLE LANGUAGES   Most data-base management systems have their own query language. For the most popular types, multiple languages are available from software houses. These languages differ substantially in their features and usability (Fig. 8.4). Different types of end users need different types of languages.

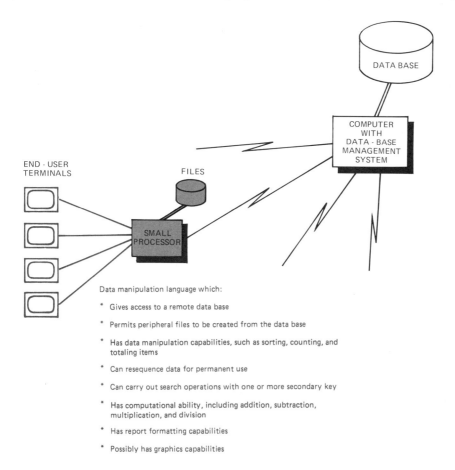

Data manipulation language which:

* Gives access to a remote data base

* Permits peripheral files to be created from the data base

* Has data manipulation capabilities, such as sorting, counting, and totaling items

* Can resequence data for permanent use

* Can carry out search operations with one or more secondary key

* Has computational ability, including addition, subtraction, multiplication, and division

* Has report formatting capabilities

* Possibly has graphics capabilities

Figure 8.3   Some systems need languages which can create peripheral files from a remote data base, and allow end users to manipulate and search those files peripherally, without endangering the integrity of performance of the remote data-base system.

FORMS-ORIENTED LANGUAGE

One of the easiest-to-use types of query language is that in which the inquirer fills in a form.

One of the query languages used with the MARK IV data-base management system (9) employs forms for query specification. Informatics Inc., who produce MARK IV, advertise: "Learn to write computer programs in five minutes!"

Figure 8.5 (pp. 82–84) gives a simple example of a MARK IV query. The form that it shows can be filled in very simply and quickly and then keypunched and processed. The user employs a simple data dictionary to tell him the names of the data items he can list on his form.

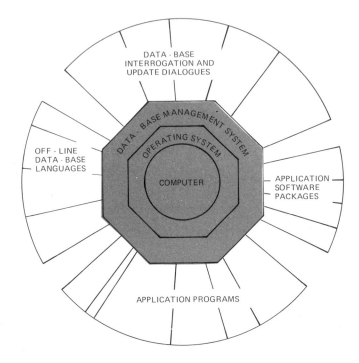

Figure 8.4 The data-base management system, like the operating system, may be that of the computer manufacturer, ensuring compatibility with his migration path; but multiple end-user languages from different sources may employ it.

The user employs a simple data dictionary to tell the names of the data items he can list on his form.

MARK IV employs many different forms, including forms for defining data structures, defining transactions used to update the files, defining logical and arithmetic operations to be performed on the data items, defining in detail the layout of reports to be generated, defining tables to be used, and cataloging the processing requests.

GIS   IBM's GIS (Generalized Information System) (10) is, in effect, a high-level programming language restricted to operations on a data base structured using the DL/I data description language. Far fewer statements are needed to carry out a set of operations than in, for example, COBOL.

The following example consists of 14 lines of GIS code. To produce the same report in COBOL would require about 250 lines of code (11).

Figure 8.6 (p. 85) shows a DL/I data base and a GIS query using that data base. Suppose that a marketing manager has been conducting a new advertising campaign. He is concerned after an intensive burst of advertising that certain warehouses may be running out of stock of product number 75438.

From the data base in Fig. 8.6 he receives monthly reports of sales and advertising expenditure. These do not tell him about the sales of the 13 days of the current month which may have been critical. He can obtain a stock status report on any product when he wants it, using a previously written inquiry program. This confirms his fear that certain warehouses may be running short. He can also check the replenishment schedule for the warehouses, and he sees that the next delivery to some warehouses is not until late next week. His staff assistant asks the data-processing manager for an urgent report showing how many days of stock are left at the current rate of sale.

The results could not be obtained sufficiently quickly using COBOL or any other conventional programming language. The GIS specialist enters the query shown in Fig. 8.6. He creates a new file, which he calls FREDFILE, and creates two new data items in it. The first, called SALERATE, shows the average rate of sale of product number 75438 over the past 13 days. The second, called DAYSLEFT, shows how many days stock are left if the item continues to sell at that rate. The printout which results from the query in Fig. 8.6 is as follows:

LOC	DAYSLEFT	SALERATE	XRATIO
ATLANTA	3	805	4.0
BOSTON	10	512	2.7
CHICAGO	15	441	1.0
HOUSTON	20	325	0.8
MILWAUKEE	12	622	2.1
NEW YORK	3	2113	2.1
SAN FRANCISCO	25	401	0.7
ST. LOUIS	4	407	3.7

On seeing the result the GIS specialist decides to add a title to the report and sort the output to show the warehouses that are running out fastest at the top of the list. He enters:

```
QUERY PRODFILE 'DEPLETION REPORT FOR PRODUCT
NUMBER 75438,' PRODNAME
SORT FREDFILE DAYSLEFT
QUERY FREDFILE
LIST RECORD
```

MARK IV, produced by Informatics Inc., is a data-base management system which permits information requests to be specified very quickly by filling in forms. MARK IV can handle complex data bases using the DL/I language, and process complex information requests. The following is a simple illustration.

An accountant has received a request from his boss for the total year-to-date activity on one vendor's account. Taking an Information Request form, the accountant writes in a Request Name. Any name that fits ①. He writes TODAY in the Report Date box (to get *today's* date on the report) ②.

No other information is required in the heading area of the form. MARK IV provides automatic default conditions for everything left blank. In this example, MARK IV will produce a detail report, single spaced, on standard 8½" by 11" paper.

To be able to request information from a file of data, the file has been defined previously to MARK IV. The file definition provides the accountant with the names of the pieces of data which make up the file. Other qualities of the data, such as size, are also provided. MARK IV stores this definition, and a printed glossary of the names is available any time for any users of the file.

Therefore, when the accountant wants to refer to the data in the file, he just looks at the glossary for the Accounts Payable file and uses the names that were assigned to the pieces of data in the file. For instance, the piece of data which is the vendor number is called VENDOR, and since the vendor in which he is interested is ABC Manufacturing (vendor number 2386), he "selects" that vendor by writing VENDOR EQ (equal) D (for Decimal) 2386 in the Record Selection area of the form. When looking at the Accounts Payable file, MARK IV will pick out only the data about vendor number 2386 ③.

And, since only activity for 1972 is of concern, the accountant writes A (for And) INVYEAR EQ D 72 to select only the activity concerning ABC Manufacturing Company that has taken place in 1972 ④.

If no such special selection criteria are required, then the Record Selection portion of the form is left blank. The default condition for this is that MARK IV will report on the total contents of the file.

Now that the accountant has specified the selection criteria, he can specify the data he wants to see on the report itself. He wants to see the vendor's invoice number, invoice date, invoice amount, check number, check date and amount paid. He writes the names for those pieces of data, one to a line and in the sequence he wants them to appear across the report, in the Report Specification section of the form ⑤.

To get a total of the activity being reported, the accountant simply enters a G (for Grand) in the column marked Total on the same lines as INV-AMT and AMT-PAID. MARK IV will provide a grand total of all the INV-AMTs and AMT-PAIDs in the report ⑥.

Finally, to give a meaningful title to his report, the accountant writes his own title in the section of the form labeled TITLE ⑦.

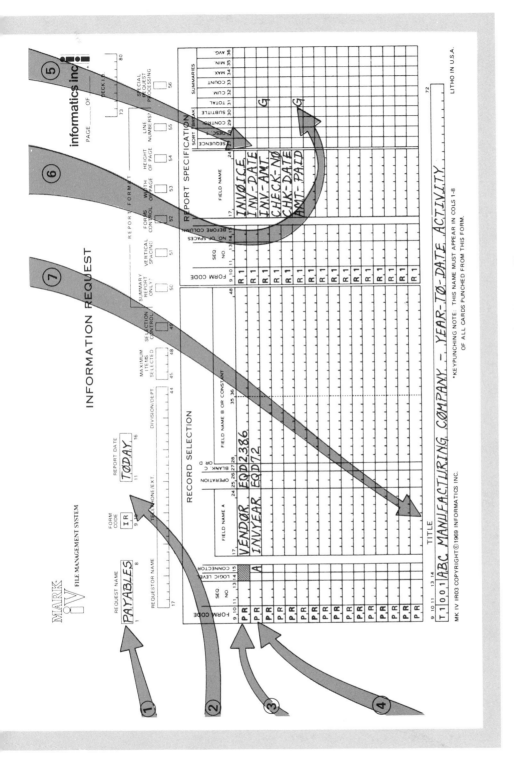

Figure 8.5 The MARK IV Information Request Form.

(continued)

The accountant will give his filled out Information Request form to someone in the data-processing organization who will have the form keypunched, put it on the computer, and deliver the resulting report as soon as it is available.

The report produced by this request is shown below:

```
04/28/72    ABC MANUFACTURING COMPANY - YEAR-TO-DATE ACTIVITY      PAGE 1
--------------------------------------------------------------------------
            INVOICE    INVOICE    INVOICE    CHECK     CHECK      AMOUNT
            NUMBER     DATE       AMOUNT     NUMBER    DATE       PAID
--------------------------------------------------------------------------
            51-03917   01/12/72        3.47  002571   02/15/72        3.47
            51-07242   01/14/72       60.43  002571   02/15/72       60.43
            51-11275   01/21/72      152.40  002571   02/15/72      152.40
            51-12336   01/27/72      104.53  002571   02/15/72      104.53
            51-14514   02/03/72       14.44  002819   03/15/72       14.44
            51-17180   02/14/72      102.42  002819   03/15/72      102.42
            51-20992   02/29/72       63.00  002819   03/15/72       63.00
            51-21541   03/02/72      189.12  002819   03/15/72      189.12
            51-23730   03/07/72       19.72  003093   04/17/72       19.72
            51-24226   03/10/72    1,092.46  003093   04/17/72    1,092.46
            51-28859   03/27/72      605.00  003093   04/17/72      605.00
            51-29331   03/31/72    5,486.00  003093   04/17/72    5,486.00
            51-31155   04/11/72       19.09
            51-33126   04/21/72      187.55
            51-34568   04/25/72       28.90

                                                             7,892.99
```

Other MARK IV forms enable the professional analyst programmer to execute more complex processing and reporting operations.

Courtesy of Informatics Inc., Canoga Park, Calif.

Figure 8.5   (Continued)

This time he obtains the following:

DEPLETION REPORT FOR PRODUCT NUMBER
75438, BEDWARMER

LOC	DAYSLEFT	SALERATE	XRATIO
ATLANTA	3	805	4.0
NEW YORK	3	2113	4.1
ST. LOUIS	4	407	3.7
BOSTON	10	512	2.7
MILWAUKEE	12	622	2.1
CHICAGO	15	441	1.0
HOUSTON	20	325	0.8
SAN FRANCISCO	25	401	0.7

A DL/I data-base description:

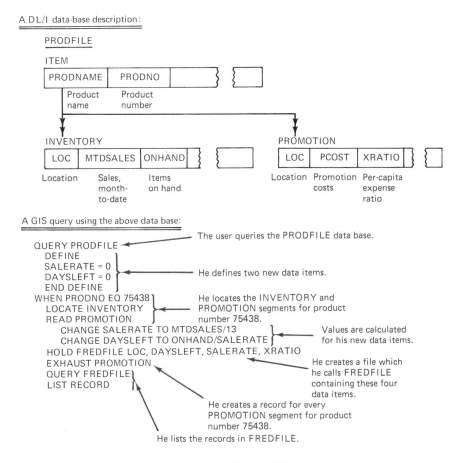

Figure 8.6 Use of GIS.

The marketing manager holds a conference and decides that some of the product should be moved from the Houston warehouse to the Atlanta warehouse, from Boston to New York, and from Chicago to St. Louis. The advertising expenditure in San Francisco is stepped up.

The GIS specialist improves his routine and his report format in anticipation of its being used again and stores it. Most decision making is rarely a one-step process. The decision maker is likely to come back with a series of refinements, a progressive reexamination of successive results. The ability to store GIS routines, report formats, and interim files and to modify them later is therefore important.

GIS has facilities for more elaborate logical and arithmetical operations. Its output can be edited and formatted as required. The user can query many segments at once, taking different data items from each, and can create many temporary or permanent files. These files, unlike that in the example, could be very large files. It does, however, need a specialist or well-trained person to use it, not a casual terminal user without training.

EASY-TO-USE DATA-BASE LANGUAGES

While languages such as GIS are easy for a programmer to use, many end users avoid them because of their seeming difficulty. However, languages can be devised, following the rules of Box 8.1, which have equivalent data manipulation capabilities.

Data-base languages which are nonprocedural and easy for users without programming skills to learn include SEQUEL (12), QUEL (13), NOMAD (14), and QUERY-BY-EXAMPLE (15, 16, 17). Of these, QUERY-BY-EXAMPLE demonstrates the simplicity that is needed for widespread end-user communication.

QUERY-BY-EXAMPLE

It is desirable that a naive user approaching a terminal should be required to know as little as possible in order to get started. He may have to know a little more in order to use the subtleties of the language, but this also should be **minimized.**

He may approach a data base knowing very little about the names of the records or fields, or how to access them. Using QUERY-BY-EXAMPLE, I have taken a secretary who had never touched computers or terminals before, and explained in the simplest terms what a data base is. Within half an hour she was using the language and manipulating the data stored. Various psychological studies of the language (16) have shown that naive users acquire the skill to make complicated queries in less than three hours. Yet QUERY-BY-EXAMPLE can accomplish anything that GIS can, and can handle some forms of query that GIS and other languages cannot.

The user sitting at the terminal is presented with the skeleton of a table on the screen, thus:

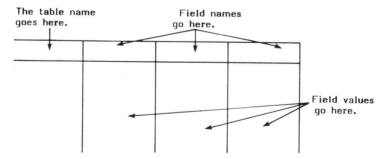

The user may fill in the spaces for table name, field name, or field value in order to express a query. He can also modify the data, or insert or delete new items.

P. stands for "print." If the user writes P in one of the spaces, he wants the machine to fill in that space.

He might want to know what fields are in the EMPLOYEE record, so he types:

EMPLOYEE	P.	P.	P.

or, in a shorter form:

EMPLOYEE P.			

The terminal may respond, increasing the number of columns as necessary:

EMPLOYEE	EMPLOYEE #	NAME	SALARY	DEPARTMENT

The SALARY field heading may not appear if the user is not authorized to see salaries.

If he wants to know what employees work in the TIN BENDING department, he types

EMPLOYEE	EMPLOYEE #	NAME	SALARY	DEPARTMENT
		P.		**TIN BENDING**

Their names are then listed in the NAME column.

This feature of the language was not implemented in its initial versions.

He may not be sure of the correct title of the TIN BENDING department, so he puts a P. in the DEPARTMENT value column:

EMPLOYEE	EMPLOYEE #	NAME	SALARY	DEPARTMENT
				P.

The terminal will then list the names of all the departments, and the user can select the one he needs.

If the user wants to know the salaries of all the employees in the TIN BEND-ING department, he enters two P's:

EMPLOYEE	EMPLOYEE #	NAME	SALARY	DEPARTMENT
		P.	P.	**TIN BENDING**

Needless to say, any such powerful end-user language must have security controls in the system to prevent users seeing data they are not authorized to see.

To obtain all the information in the EMPLOYEE record about employees in the TIN BENDING department, he can write

EMPLOYEE	EMPLOYEE #	NAME	SALARY	DEPARTMENT
P.				**TIN BENDING**

The machine will then fill in the whole skeleton for the TIN BENDING department.

The user may be interested in SALARY values, but he does not know which record contains salaries. He can write SALARY in the empty skeleton, and a P. in the table name position:

P.	SALARY		

It does not matter which column heading SALARY is written in. The machine displays the name of the tables, or names of several tables, which contain a field called SALARY.

Even more basic, the beginner might simply print P. in the table name position:

P.			

The machine then displays the names of **all tables which the user is allowed to see (within whatever security constraints exist).**

UNKNOWLEDGEABLE BEGINNERS   It will be seen that the user can approach this dialogue with no knowledge of either computer languages or the contents of the data base. He need not even know the names of any tables or fields in the data base. Yet five minutes after first sitting at the terminal he can be making enquiries, even enquiries which would be fairly complex in other languages, such as "List all employees with a training in cost accounting who joined the company before 1975 and are earning more than 20,000."

EMPLOYEE	EMPLOYEE #	NAME	SALARY	DEPT	YEAR OF HIRE	TRAINING
P.			>20000		<1975	ACCOUNTING

Here he is using the operators **greater than** and **less than** (> and <). He may use any of the following inequality operators: ≠, >, > =, <, and < =, ≠ can be replaced by ⌐ or ⌐= .

The user may have more columns than he needs on the screen (especially if the width of the display exceeds the width of the screen). He may blank out some of the column headings and reenter his request. The result omits the unwanted columns.

UPDATES   The user may be permitted to update certain fields. The update operator is "U." If he wants to increase WEINBURG's salary to 21,000, he may type "U" and "21,000" as follows:

EMPLOYEE	EMPLOYEE #	NAME	SALARY
		FLANAGON J E	
		SNOOK S	
U.		WEINBURG G	21000

Here security is even more important. The system must make it impossible for users to make unauthorized changes.

ARITHMETIC The user can employ arithmetic operators. For example, he may want to increase WEINBURG's salary by 10%. He can do this as follows:

EMPLOYEE	EMPLOYEE #	NAME	SALARY
		WEINBURG G	20397

EMPLOYEE	EMPLOYEE #	NAME	SALARY
U.		WEINBURG G	20397 **x 1.1**

The machine responds by placing the updated amount in the SALARY field— 22436.70.

EXAMPLES With some of the more elaborate types of query, the user gives an **example** of the results he wants. In doing so he may type a value which is not an actual value but a made-up value. He indicates that it is a made-up **example** of a value by underlining it.

To illustrate this, suppose that the user was not permitted to know WEINBURG's salary, but nevertheless wanted to update it by 10%. He would type an example of what the salary might be, for example 500. 500 is invented. It does not matter how far from actuality it is. The update is done as follows:

EMPLOYEE	EMPLOYEE #	NAME	SALARY
U.		WEINBURG G	500 x 1.1

The machine indicates that the salary field has been updated.

The use of examples permits many fields to be changed with one instruction. Thus everybody in the TIN BENDING department could be given a salary increase of 200 as follows:

EMPLOYEE	EMPLOYEE #	NAME	SALARY	DEPARTMENT
U.			500 + 200	**TIN BENDING**

"200" is real, so it is not underlined. "500" is a guess, so it is underlined.

These two types of entries, real and imaginary, can be placed anywhere in the skeleton.

Partial underlines are also permitted. For example "WONG" or "WX" might by typed in the NAME column. This would mean that W is real, the other letters are imaginary. It would refer to all names beginning with "W." Similarly, "WENDY" is an example referring to all names beginning with "WE." If he does not know WEINBURG's initials, he might type "WEINBURG X." Similarly, "20000" means all numbers ending with "000." (This feature was also not implemented on the initial versions of the language.)

MORE COMPLEX
QUERIES

More complex queries are possible in which the user enters more than one row into the skeleton. The rows are linked by **examples.**

The user may have the following query: "Find the names of all employees who earn more than WEINBURG." He can guess a value for WEINBURG's salary, say 700. He then makes an entry requesting the names of employees who earn more than this value 700:

EMPLOYEE	NAME	SALARY
	WEINBURG	700
	P.	>700

It does not matter what value is entered as the example. A user familiar with the system might enter:

EMPLOYEE	NAME	SALARY
	WEINBURG	X
	P.	> X

The user might want to ask the question "Which employees earn more than their manager?" Using the table

EMPLOYEE	NAME	MANAGER	SALARY

the user types an example of the result that he wants. Print the names of employees who work for FRED, let us say, and earn more than 700 (also an example), when FRED earns 700:

EMPLOYEE	NAME	MANAGER	SALARY
	P.	FRED	>700
	FRED		700

The names of employees who earn more than their manager will be printed.

The cautious user may want to check that the result is what he wanted, so he might display the salaries in question. If WEINBURG's name is in the result, he might verify it by entering.

EMPLOYEE	NAME	MANAGER	SALARY
	WEINBURG	Z	P.
	Z P.		P.

The name of WEINBURG's manager will be printed and the salaries of both of them.

The user might want to ask, "Does anyone earn more than the salaries of WEINBURG and FLANAGAN combined?" Let us imagine that WEINBURG earns 2000 and FLANAGAN earns 3000:

EMPLOYEE	NAME	MANAGER	SALARY
	WEINBURG		2000
	FLANAGAN		3000
	P.		>(2000 + 3000)

IMPLICIT AND and OR

To display all employees in the TIN BENDING department with a salary between 2000 and 3000, the skeleton is filled in as follows:

EMPLOYEE	NAME	SALARY	DEPARTMENT
	P. FRED	**>2000**	**TIN BENDING**
	FRED	**<3000**	

This request contains an AND condition:

$$(SALARY > 2000) \textbf{ AND } (SALARY < 3000).$$

The AND condition is implicit in the way the skeleton is filled in. Similarly, an OR condition can be implicit. For example, "Display all employees earning more than 2000 who work in either the TIN BENDING or MILLING departments":

EMPLOYEE	NAME	SALARY	DEPARTMENT
	P.	**>2000**	**TIN BENDING**
	P.	**>2000**	**MILLING**

LINKS BETWEEN TABLES

The user's query often cannot be answered by reference to one type of record. It requires data in more than one record. With QUERY-BY-EXAMPLE it would require more than one table.

Often, management perceive their data-processing installation as being inflexible because their queries cannot be answered. The data to answer them are scattered through more than one type of record. Data-base management technology seeks to solve this problem by providing appropriate links between records.

The QUERY-BY-EXAMPLE user can display two or more different skeletons on the screen at once. He fills in both of them and then presses the ENTER key (or equivalent) indicating that this is one entry.

The skeletons we have shown above do not show who is the manager of the TIN BENDING department. Suppose that this information is given in a separate table, as follows:

DEPARTMENT	DEPT NAME	LOCATION	MANAGER

The user wants to know the salary of the manager of the TIN BENDING department. He enters the following query, using the example "FRED" to link the two tables:

DEPARTMENT	DEPT NAME	LOCATION	MANAGER
	TIN BENDING		**FRED**

EMPLOYEE	NAME	SALARY
	FRED	**P.**

The machine will print the salary of the manager of the TIN BENDING department.

The language is designed with the excellent principle that the thinking process the user follows is that which he would use to find the same information without a computer. Suppose that he had to answer the foregoing query with a set of printed tables. He would first look up who is the manager of the TIN BENDING department and then look up his salary.

Suppose that the manufacturing of a product requires operations to be done in several departments as shown in the shop-floor routing record:

SHOP FLOOR ROUTING	PART #	OPERATION #	OPERATION TYPE	DEPARTMENT

One location has several departments in it, and the query must be answered: "What parts have operations performed in the location XYZ?" Using manual tables, the user might look up what departments exist in the location XYZ, and then what parts have operations in those departments. With QUERY-BY-EXAMPLE he would do the same, as follows:

DEPARTMENT	DEPT NAME	LOCATION	MANAGER
	MILLING	**XYZ**	

SHOP FLOOR ROUTING	PART #	OPERATION #	OPERATION TYPE	DEPARTMENT
	P.			**MILLING**

FUNCTIONS   QUERY-BY-EXAMPLE has a number of built-in functions. These are represented by mnemonics such as the following:

SUM:	Sum of the values
CNT:	Count of the values
AVG:	Average of a set values
MAX:	Maximum value
MIN:	Minimum value
UN:	Unique values; that is, the values in a set, excluding duplicates

The average salary in the TIN BENDING department is found as follows:

EMPLOYEE	EMPLOYEE #	SALARY	DEPARTMENT
		P. AVG	**TIN BENDING**

The department whose manager has the maximum salary can be found as follows:

DEPARTMENT	DEPT. NAME	MANAGER
	X P.	**FRED**

EMPLOYEE	NAME	SALARY
	FRED	**MAX**

Again the user is formulating the query in the same way that he would do it manually. He would look up the manager of each department, then look up his salary, and find the maximum salary. He could ask the machine to display the maximum salary by typing P. MAX in the salary column.

The user is not completely free of mnemonics because of the foregoing functions. However, a beginner does need them. To avoid the need to remember mnemonics, the functions could be on specially labeled keys.

**USE OF A
CONDITION BOX**

In addition to displaying one or more table skeletons, as described above, the user can display another two-dimensional object called a CONDITION BOX:

The user can display this condition box at any time he wants. He uses it to display conditions which are difficult to express in the tables. For example, the query "Display all employees earning more than 2000 who work in either the TIN BENDING or MILLING departments" could be expressed as follows:

EMPLOYEE	NAME	SALARY	DEPARTMENT
	P.	$\underline{S}$	$\underline{D}$

CONDITIONS
$\underline{D}$ = (MILLING/TIN BENDING)
$\underline{S}$ = > 2000

Multiple conditions can be listed in this way relating to one query.

**INSERTIONS AND
DELETIONS**

The QUERY-BY-EXAMPLE user can insert new entries into the tables, or delete entries (with appropriate security constraints).

Insertions and deletions are done in the same style as query operations except that "I" is used instead of "P" for insertions, and "D" is used for deletions. To insert a new employee record, the user calls up the EMPLOYEE skeleton and fills it in:

EMPLOYEE	EMPLOYEE #	NAME	SALARY	MANAGER	DEPARTMENT
I.	27511	BONTEMPO C	8000	MORTON A	SYSTEMS

Similarly, an employee record can be deleted:

EMPLOYEE	EMPLOYEE #	NAME	SALARY	MANAGER	DEPARTMENT
D.	27511	BONTEMPO C	8000	MORTON A	SYSTEMS

All employees in the SYSTEMS department may be deleted as follows:

EMPLOYEE	EMPLOYEE #	NAME	SALARY	MANAGER	DEPARTMENT
D.					**SYSTEMS**

Similarly, the user can create a new table or add a new field to an existing table. The language permits him to create a new table from existing tables which is either a **snapshot** or a **view.** A snapshot merely contains the values of the data as they were at the time of its creation. A view is a table which will be dynamically updated to reflect changes in the base tables.

USERS' OWN TABLES   Users can thus create their own tables and manipulate them as they wish. They can sort the tables or request that a result be displayed sorted. For this there are two mnemonics: AO (Ascending Order) and DO (Descending Order). For example, the employees in the TIN BENDING department can be displayed in alphabetical order:

EMPLOYEE	EMPLOYEE #	NAME	DEPARTMENT
		P.AO	**TIN BENDING**

All employees could be displayed with other details in order of descending salary:

EMPLOYEE	EMPLOYEE #	NAME	MANAGER	SALARY	DEPARTMENT
P.				P. DO	

Users can store such files for their own reference, giving them a new table name if they wish. Suppose that a user wants a table called "EMP" which gives the employees at each location, the locations being in ascending order and employees being in order of descending salary within each location.

He might fill in the skeletons as follows:

I. EMP	LOCATION	EMPLOYEE #	NAME	SALARY
I.	AO(1).NEW YORK	52	FRED	DO(2).500

EMPLOYEE	NAME	DEPT. NAME	SALARY
	FRED	MILLING	500

DEPARTMENT	DEPT. NAME	LOCATION
	MILLING	NEW YORK

Where there is a major and minor sort, as above, AO (1) or DO (1) refers to the major sort and AO (2) or DO (2) to the minor sort.

COMPARISON WITH COBOL

Figure 8.7 gives a very simple COBOL program for answering a query using IBM's IMS facilities (18). The input message contains HOSPITAL NAME and WARD NUMBER as follows:

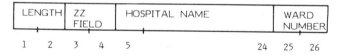

LENGTH	ZZ FIELD	HOSPITAL NAME	WARD NUMBER

1   2   3   4   5   24   25   26

(The LENGTH and ZZ fields are control fields required by the software. The ZZ field is unused here: it is employed on some output messages to indicate where a message should be displayed on a screen.)

The COBOL program responds to this input by returning a message with HOSPITAL NAME and WARD NUMBER for confirmation and then sending messages listing the patients in that ward and their bed numbers, thus:

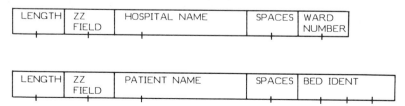

LENGTH	ZZ FIELD	HOSPITAL NAME	SPACES	WARD NUMBER

LENGTH	ZZ FIELD	PATIENT NAME	SPACES	BED IDENT

```
000100 ID DIVISION.
000200 PROGRAM-ID. CHAP11.
000300 AUTHOR. JOSEPH F. LEBEN.
000400 DATE-COMPILED.
000500
000600 REMARKS. THIS IS A VERY SIMPLE IMS/DC PROGAM. IT DOES VERY
000700         LITTLE ERROR CHECKING.  IT READS AN INPUT TRANSACTION
000800         WHICH HAS THE FOLLOWING FORMAT:
000900         FORMAT.
001000           POSITIONS   1 -  2   TRANSACTION LENGTH
001100                       3 -  4   ZZ FIELD
001200                       5 - 24   HOSPITAL NAME
001300                      25 - 26   WARD NUMBER
001400
001500         FOR EACH TRANSACTION, THE PROGRAM SENDS A CONFIRMING
001600         MESSAGE BACK TO THE TERMINAL REPEATING THE HOSPITAL NAME
001700         AND WARD NUMBER, AND THEN LISTS OUT ALL THE PATIENT
001800         SEGMENTS UNDER THAT WARD AND HOSPITAL.
001900
002000 ENVIRONMENT DIVISION.
002100 CONFIGURATION SECTION.
002200 SOURCE-COMPUTER. IBM-370-168.
002300 OBJECT-COMPUTER. IBM-370-168.
002400     EJECT
002500 DATA DIVISION.
002600
002700 WORKING-STORAGE SECTION.
002800
002900 01   TERM-IN.
003000
003100      03   IN-LENGTH              PIC S9999    COMP.
003200      03   IN-ZZ                 PIC XX.
003300      03   HOSPNAME-TERM         PIC X(20).
003400      03   WARDNO-TERM           PIC XX.
003500
003600 01   TERM-OUT-PATIENT-HOSPITAL.
003700
003800      03   OUT-LENGTH            PIC S9999    VALUE +30 COMP.
003900      03   OUT-ZZ               PIC XX       VALUE SPACE.
004000      03   HOSPITAL-INFO        PIC X(20).
004100      03   FILLER               PIC X(4)     VALUE SPACE.
004200      03   WARD-INFO            PIC XX.
004300
004400 01   TERM-OUT-PATIENT.
004500
004600      03   OUT-LENGTH            PIC S9999    VALUE +129 COMP.
004700      03   OUT-ZZ               PIC XX.
004800      03   PATIENT-INFO         PIC X(125).
004900 01   GET-NEXT-P               PIC X(4)     VALUE 'GNP '.
005000 01   GET-UNIQUE               PIC X(4)     VALUE 'GU  '.
005100 01   INSERT-FUNC              PIC X(4)     VALUE 'ISRT'.
005200 01   P-Z-D                    PIC X        VALUE SPACE.
005210 01   P-Z-D-2 REDEFINES P-Z-D.
005211      03   PACKED-ZERO         PIC S9.
005300 01   PACKED-ONE              PIC S9       VALUE +1.
005400
```

(*Continued on the next two pages*)

Figure 8.7 An example of a COBOL program for an inquiry (18). The same inquiry can be handled with one simple screen of QUERY-BY-EXAMPLE.

```
005500 01  HOSPITAL-SSA.
005600     03  FILLER          PIC X(21)  VALUE 'HOSPITAL*D(HOSPNAME =',
005700     03  HOSPNAME-SSA    PIC X(20),
005800     03  FILLER          PIC X      VALUE ')'.
005900
006000 01  WARD-SSA.
006100     03  FILLER          PIC X(19)  VALUE 'WARD    (WARDNO  =',
006200     03  WARDNO-SSA      PIC X(2).
006300     03  FILLER          PIC X      VALUE ')'.
006400
006500 01  PATIENT-SSA         PIC  X(9)  VALUE 'PATIENT  '.
006900     EJECT
007000 01  I-O-AREA COPY PATIENT.
007100
007200 01  HOSPITAL-INPUT.
007300     03  HOSPITAL.
007400         05  HOSPNAME        PIC X(20).
007500         05  HOSP-ADDRESS    PIC X(30).
007600         05  HOSP-PHONE      PIC X(10).
007700     03  WARD.
007800         05  WARDNO          PIC XX.
007900         05  TOT-ROOMS       PIC XXX.
008000         05  TOT-BEDS        PIC XXX.
008100         05  BEDAVAIL        PIC XXX.
008200         05  WARDTYPE        PIC X(20).
008300
008400 LINKAGE SECTION.
008500 01  DB-PCB    COPY MASKC.
008600
008700 01  I-O-PCB.
008800     03  LTERM-NAME      PIC X(8).
008900     03  FILLER          PIC XX.
009000     03  I-O-STAT-CODE   PIC XX.
009100     03  INPUT-PREFIX.
009200         05  PREF-DATE       PIC S9(7)   COMP-3.
009300         05  PREF-TIME       PIC S9(7)   COMP-3.
009310         05  PREF-SEQ        PIC S9(7)   COMP.
009500 PROCEDURE DIVISION.
009600
009700 START-OF-PROGRAM.
009800
009900     ENTRY 'DLITCBL' USING I-O-PCB DB-PCB.
010000     PERFORM GET-MESSAGE THRU GET-MESSAGE-EXIT
010010                     UNTIL I-O-STAT-CODE EQUAL 'QC' OR 'QD'.
010100     GOBACK.
010200
010300 GET-MESSAGE.
010400
010500     CALL 'CBLTDLI' USING GET-UNIQUE
010600                     I-O-PCB
010700                     TERM-IN.
010800
010900     IF I-O-STAT-CODE EQUAL 'QC'          GO TO GET-MESSAGE-EXIT.
011000     IF I-O-STAT-CODE NOT EQUAL SPACE
011100
011200         MOVE I-O-PCB TO PATIENT-INFO
011300         PERFORM SEND-PAT-RTN
011400         MOVE SPACE TO PATIENT-INFO
011500         GO TO GET-MESSAGE-EXIT.
011600
011700     MOVE HOSPNAME-TERM   TO HOSPNAME-SSA.
```

Figure 8.7   (Continued)

100

```
011800        MOVE WARDNO-TERM        TO WARDNO-SSA.
011900
012000        CALL 'CBLTDLI' USING GET-UNIQUE
012100                               DB-PCB
012200                               HOSPITAL-INPUT
012300                               HOSPITAL-SSA
012400                               WARD-SSA.
012500
012600        IF STATUS-CODE NOT EQUAL SPACE
012610
012700            MOVE 'NO-HOSPITAL OR WARD' TO PATIENT-INFO
012800            PERFORM SEND-PAT-RTN
012810            MOVE SPACE TO PATIENT-INFO.
012900            GO TO GET-MESSAGE-EXIT.
013000
013100        MOVE HOSPNAME TO HOSPITAL-INFO.
013200        MOVE WARDNO   TO WARD-INFO.
013300
013400        CALL 'CBLTDLI' USING INSERT-FUNC
013500                               I-O-PCB
013600                               TERM-OUT-PATIENT-HOSPITAL.
013700
013800        IF I-O-STAT-CODE NOT EQUAL SPACE
013900            GO TO DUMP-IT.
014000        PERFORM GET-PATIENT THRU GET-PATIENT-EXIT
014010                               UNTIL STATUS-CODE EQUAL  GE .
014100
014200 GET-MESSAGE-EXIT.
014300        EXIT.
014500 GET-PATIENT.
014600
014700        CALL 'CBLTDLI' USING GET-NEXT-P
014800                               DB-PCB
014900                               I-O-AREA
015000                               PATIENT-SSA.
015100
015200        IF STATUS-CODE EQUAL 'GE' GO TO GET-PATIENT-EXIT.
015300        IF STATUS-CODE NOT EQUAL SPACE
015400
015500            MOVE DB-PCB TO TERM-OUT-PATIENT
015600            PERFORM SEND-PAT-RTN
015700            MOVE SPACE TO TERM-OUT-PATIENT
015800            GO TO GET-MESSAGE.
015900
016000        PERFORM SEND-PAT-RTN.
016100
016200 GET-PATIENT-EXIT.
016300        EXIT.
016400
016500 SEND-PAT-RTN.
016600
016700        CALL 'CBLTDLI' USING INSERT-FUNC
016800                               I-O-PCB
016900                               TERM-OUT-PATIENT.
017000
017100        IF I-O-STAT-CODE NOT EQUAL SPACE
017200            GO TO DUMP-IT.
017300
017400 DUMP-IT.
017500
017700        ADD PACKED-ONE TO PACKED-ZERO.
```

Figure 8.7 (Continued)

The entire COBOL program could be replaced by the use of a simple data-base query language. In QUERY-BY-EXAMPLE a skeleton might be filled in as follows:

PATIENT	PAT NAME	HOSP NAME	WARD NO	BED IDENT
		GREENWICH	24	

A typical rate of COBOL programming is about 30 lines of code per person-day (including debugging and documentation). Given the alternative, programming like that in Fig. 8.7 is horrifyingly expensive and inflexible. Worse, such a technique for computer usage prevents most would-be users from employing the data bases.

DISTRIBUTED
DATA BASES

There is much to be said for certain types of end users having a local data-base machine containing their own data. They can create these data from those which exist in a larger machine, possibly a distant production-oriented machine. Easy-to-use languages, like QUERY-BY-EXAMPLE could enable them to both extract the data they want from a larger data base, and manipulate them.

It will always be true that powerful data-base languages or information retrieval languages give users the capability to make requests which would be expensive in machine time. Too many such requests might play havoc with the performance of a central machine. The users should be warned if their request is inappropriate. (STAIRS information retrieval software, for example, warns the user of the number of occurrences of records relating to a given request before the user tells the machine to execute the request.) If the users' data are in a peripheral machine, the users can be in control of their own costs, freed from scheduling constraints of a central computer, and will not endanger the performance of the central machine.

The most important thing that QUERY-BY-EXAMPLE demonstrates in its working installations is that a powerful data-base language for end users can be very easy to use. Naive, unskilled users who have never touched terminals before can come to grips with the language very quickly. No English phrases are used, so the naive user is not tempted to enter English, which the machine cannot interpret. A manager who rarely goes near a terminal and who instantly forgets mnemonics can walk up to a QUERY-BY-EXAMPLE terminal and extract information from it.

For most (but not all) end users there is simply no need for the language to be more complex. The difficulties of GIS-like languages, and the scope for making invalid statements in English-like languages, are **major disincentives** to users who should be employing data bases but are frightened of the terminal dialogues.

Those software houses and manufacturers who understand this and who market products which overcome ordinary users' fears of terminals have vast sales ahead. They can put appropriate user dialogues into small peripheral machines, regardless of what happens in large, distant machines which may update and manage the data.

There are many different types of end-user data-base languages and the diversity will probably increase. Different types of users have very different needs and skills. A language which is good for one is not good for them all. There needs to be different languages to meet different needs.

9 OWNERSHIP OF DATA, AND PRIVACY

OWNERSHIP OF DATA A major concern of data-base end users is: "Who *owns* the data?"

In a **file** environment it is usually clear who owns the files. Data base is different because many types of users share the data. Who owns it in this case? Does the central data-processing department own it? Has a user who once owned his own files lost control of them?

The word "own" is itself imprecise in this context. There are several separate attributes to ownership. We can replace the ownership question with the following questions:

1. Who is responsible for the accuracy of the data?
2. Who is permitted to update the data?
3. Who is permitted to read and use the data (without necessarily being permitted to change it)?
4. Who is responsible for determining who can read and update the data?
5. Who controls the security of the data?

Each data-item group or each data item can be separately controlled so that only authorized users can read it or change it. A good data-base management system has the capability to enforce tight security control of this type. The system designer must then define who is permitted to read and update the data. It is usually desirable that **only one** person or department should be able to change a given data item or data-item group. If more than one can change it, then it is more difficult to control integrity. There are exceptions to this. For example, many branch banks may have access to a customer's central record and can debit or credit transactions to it. In this case careful central auditing controls are essential and must be thorough. The branch which holds the customer's account has the final responsibility for its accuracy.

In many cases one department enters a certain type of data. It creates the records and updates them. It is responsible for their accuracy. Although these data are extensively shared, no other department or individual is permitted to change them.

Good security is extremely important in this environment. The data must be effectively locked to prevent unauthorized reading and updating. There are many different ways of subverting a computer system and equally many safeguards to prevent it. A security officer is needed who applies the safeguards and enforces their use. The security officer is normally part of a central DP organization, not part of individual user departments.

Given that tight security is enforceable, who should decide **what** individual users are authorized to see **what** data, and to update **what** data? This decision is part of the overall system design. How the data are used, and who uses them, needs to be negotiated when the data bases are being planned. Some end users should be involved in this planning, especially when they have concerns about the sharing of data which they previously owned.

The central DP organization is often the **custodian** of the data. In a distributed environment there may be distributed custodians. Being a **custodian** of data is quite different from being their **owner.** A bank manager is the custodian of what is in his bank vault, but he does not own it. The DP department is responsible for safekeeping and controlling the data. The data may be **used** by any persons or departments to whom authority is given. They may be **updated** by one or more authorized persons.

The custodian of data knows what types of data items exist, but does not know their individual values. He knows that the payroll record contains a SALARY data item, but he does not know the value recorded in this data item; indeed, he is specifically locked out of that data item so that he cannot read it. However, if the SALARY data item must be expanded from six to seven digits, only the custodian of the data can accomplish this change.

Auditing the data usage may be a responsibility of the custodian, but generally auditors external to the custodian department are needed. A bank manager should be audited by authorities outside the bank.

In a simple file environment the "owner" of the data may have done all of these functions. In the data-base environment there may be a separate:

1. Custodian of the data

2. Security authority for the data

3. Auditor of the data

4. Persons permitted to read or use the data

5. Persons permitted to create or update the data

Who exactly can do what to what data is a basic set of decisions that should be made when the system is designed. This usage of data can be repeatedly reviewed. Details of who is authorized to read and update what data items may be recorded in the data dictionary. At a minimum, details of persons permitted to create and update the data should be recorded.

SECURITY   Somewhat related to the question of ownership, users worry if data-base systems can really be trusted. Are they really secure? Or could some unauthorized user harm the data?

It is important to understand that computer data **can** be made highly secure. Data can be locked up in a computer as securely as money can be locked up in a bank vault. Often, however, they are not. Tight security adds slightly to total system cost and could make a system slightly less convenient to use. End users, auditors, systems analysts, and the data-base designer may all participate in determining the degree of security protection, and the specific locks that are used with the data.

With the spread of high-level data-base languages, security and auditability become major concerns. Some of these languages are designed to be very easy to use. They can be used from terminals anywhere in a corporation or even outside it if appropriate security constraints are not applied. It is clear that widespread use of a language like QUERY-BY-EXAMPLE described in Chapter 8 would be dangerous if rigorous security and auditability controls were not in force.

The information stored is sometimes of great value to a corporation. It must not be lost or stolen. The more vital the information in data bases becomes, the more important it is to protect it from hardware or software failures, from catastrophes, and from criminals, vandals, incompetents, and people who misuse it.

Data security refers to protection of data against accidental or intentional disclosure to unauthorized persons or unauthorized modifications or destruction.

Privacy refers to the rights of individuals and organizations to determine for themselves when, how, and to what extent information about them is to be transmitted to others.

Although the technology of privacy is closely related to that of security, privacy is an issue that goes far beyond the computer center. To a large extent it is a problem of society. To preserve the privacy of data about individuals, solutions are needed beyond the technical solutions. Future society, dependent on a massive use of data banks, will need new legal and social controls if the degree of privacy of personal information that is cherished today is to be maintained.

It is more difficult to protect data in a data base than to protect data in the earlier systems of separate files. A file on tape usually has one owner and is accessed by one set of application programs. One person can be made responsible for what happens to it. Data in a data base may be used for many different applications by many different people and may have no one clearly defined owner. The controls to prevent unauthorized access to data are therefore more intricate and are closely bound up with the data-base management software. Nevertheless, those data-base systems for which the security precautions have been designed with care are usually more secure than their separate-file predecessors.

Security is a highly complex subject because there are so many aspects to it. A systems analyst responsible for the design of security needs to be familiar with all features of the system because the system can be attacked or security breached in highly diverse ways. Sometimes a great amount of effort is put into one aspect of security and other aspects are neglected.

If a moat is seen as the way to make a castle secure, a great amount of security engineering could be applied to the moat. It could be very wide and full of hungry piranha fish, and could have a fiercely guarded drawbridge. However, this alone would not make the castle secure. A determined intruder could tunnel under the moat. A security designer sometimes becomes so involved with one aspect of security design that he fails to see other ways of breaking into the system. It takes much knowledge and ingenuity to see all the possible ways.

TWELVE ESSENTIALS   Box 9.1 lists twelve essentials of data-base security.

1. The users of a network must be positively **identifiable** before they use it.

2. The systems and possibly also the network management must be able to check that their actions are **authorized.**

3. Their actions should be **monitored** so that if they do something wrong they are likely to be found out.

4. Data, hardware, and software should be **protected** from fire, theft, or other forms of destruction.

5. They should be **locked** from unauthorized use.

6. The data should be **reconstructible** because, however good the precautions, accidents sometimes happen.

7. The data should be **auditable.** Failure to audit computer systems adequately has permitted some of the world's largest crimes.

8. The network and systems should be **tamperproof.** Ingenious programmers should not be able to bypass the controls.

9. Transmission should be **failsafe** so that when errors or failures occur messages are not lost, double-processed, or irrecoverably garbled.

10. Transmissions should be **private,** with some being protected from eavesdropping and tampering by cryptography.

11. Computer centers should as far as possible be **catastrophe-proof.**

BOX 9.1

The Essence of Security

System users should be

- IDENTIFIABLE

Their actions should be

- AUTHORIZED
- MONITORED

Data, hardware, and software should be

- PROTECTED
- LOCKED

Data should be

- RECONSTRUCTIBLE
- AUDITABLE
- TAMPERPROOF

Transmission should be

- FAILSAFE
- PRIVATE

Vital computer centers should be

- CATASTROPHE-PROOF
- REPLICATED

12. The system should not depend on one exceptionally vital center because it might be destroyed by fire or other disaster. Such a computer center should be **replicated**. Many corporations now have a second computer center.

LAYERS OF PROTECTION   The nucleus of security control lies in the design of the computer system and its programs. Without tight controls in the hardware and software, no other precautions can make the system secure.

Design of a tightly controlled computer system, however, is not enough by itself. As indicated in Fig. 9.1, it must be surrounded by layers of control external to the system design. The layer of technical controls is surrounded by that of physical security. This refers to locks on the doors, guards, alarms, and other means of preventing unauthorized access, fire precautions, protection of stored data files, and so forth. It is not enough to have good hardware and software if disks can be stolen or the tape library destroyed by fire.

The next layer is that of administrative controls to ensure that the system is used correctly. The programmers and data-processing staff must be controlled so that they do not misuse the system. Controlled computer-room and program-testing procedures must be enforced. The administrative controls extend beyond the data-processing section to the user departments, scattered far across the network, the auditors, and general management.

The layers in Fig. 9.1 are not entirely separate. Physical security is not irrelevant when designing system techniques. The question of what data volumes should be stored off the premises affects both system design and physical security.

The administrative procedures are very closely related to the system design, especially with a real-time or terminal-based system. The auditors need to be involved in the system design, and the views of general management concerning security very much affect the system design.

The outermost layer of Fig. 9.1 is by far the most problematical. When the computer and telecommunications revolution has run its full course (and today it is only just beginning) society will be very different. Many controls will no doubt have

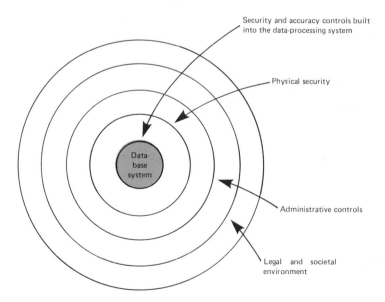

Figure 9.1　Four layers of control needed for data-base security and privacy.

evolved, seeking to maximize the benefits and minimize the dangers of a technology
of which George Orwell never dreamed. A legal framework is beginning to emerge
in some countries which will relate to computers and networks.

TYPES OF   Box 9.2 lists some of the main types of security ex-
SECURITY EXPOSURE   posure. The diversity of the list will indicate that many
                                different forms of protection are needed to make data
secure.

Catastrophes such as fire and major embezzlements have resulted in dramatic
headlines, but by far the most common and probable causes of computer calamities
are human carelessness and accidents. Carelessness has sometimes had spectacular
results. One company reported "a $2.8 million deficiency" caused by an error in
cutover. Usually, however, failures are less spectacular and more frequent.

A security program must therefore be designed to protect an installation both
from calamitous events that rarely occur and from relatively minor events, such as
damage to individual records, which occur on some systems several times a week.

BOX 9.2   Types of data-base security exposure

Type of Exposure	Inability to Process	Loss of an Entire File	Loss of Single Records	Modification of Records	Unauthorized Reading or Copying
Acts of God					
Fire, flood _____	✓	✓			
Other catastrophe _____	✓	✓			
Mechanical failure					
Computer outage _____	✓				
File unit damages disk track ____				✓	
Tape unit damages part of tape __				✓	
Disk, or other volume, un- readable _____		✓			

Continued

Box 9.2 *Continued*

Type of Exposure	Inability to Process	Loss of an Entire File	Loss of Single Records	Modification of Records	Unauthorized Reading or Copyring
Hardware/software error damages file		✓	✓	✓	
Data transmission error not detected			✓	✓	
Card (or other input) chewed up by machine			✓	✓	
Error in application program damaged record			✓	✓	
Human carelessness					
Keypunch error			✓	✓	
Terminal operator input error			✓	✓	
Computer operator error		✓	✓	✓	
Wrong volume mounted and updated	✓	✓		✓	
Wrong version of program used		✓		✓	
Accident during program testing		✓	✓	✓	
Mislaid tape or disk		✓			
Physical damage to tape or disk		✓	✓		
Malicious damage					
Looting	✓	✓			
Violent sabotage	✓	✓			
Nonviolent sabotage (e.g., tape erasure)	✓	✓	✓	✓	
Malicious computer operator		✓	✓	✓	
Malicious programmer		✓	✓	✓	
Malicious tape librarian		✓			

Box 9.2 *Continued*

Type of Exposure	Inability to Process	Loss of an Entire File	Loss of Single Records	Modification of Records	Unauthorized Reading or Copying
Malicious terminal operator		✓	✓	✓	
Malicious user (e.g., user who punches holes in returnable card)			✓	✓	
Playful malignancy (e.g., misusing terminal for fun)	✓	✓	✓	✓	✓
Crime					
Embezzlement			✓	✓	✓
Industrial espionage					✓
Employees selling commercial secrets					✓
Employees selling data for mailing lists					✓
Data bank information used for bribery or extortion					✓
Invasion of privacy					
Casual curiosity (e.g., looking up employee salaries)					✓
Looking up data of a competing corporation					✓
Obtaining personal information for political or legal reasons					✓
Nondeliberate revealing of private information					✓
Malicious invasion of privacy					✓

THREE-LEVEL ATTACK   Each security exposure must be attacked in three ways:

1. **Minimize the probability of it happening at all.** A major part of fire precautions should be preventive, and this is just as important with all other security breaches. Would-be embezzlers should be discouraged from ever beginning.

2. **Minimize the damage if it does happen.** An intruder who succeeds in bypassing the physical or programmed controls that were intended to keep him out should still be very restricted in what he can accomplish. Once started, a fire should be prevented from spreading. A disk that has been dropped and bent should be prevented from damaging a read head, which in turn could damage other disks. If the security procedures are compromised, it must be possible to limit the harm that could result. Some security designers have made the grave error of supposing that their preventive measures will always work.

3. **Design a method of recovering from the damage.** It **must** be possible to reconstruct vital records or whole files if they become accidentally or willfully damaged or lost. It **must** be possible to recover from a disastrous fire sufficiently quickly to keep the business running. If an unauthorized person obtains a security code or a file of security codes, it must be possible to change these quickly so that they are of no use to him. It is important to attack the security problem in **depth,** and recovery procedures are vital to the overall plan. The designers of the preventive mechanisms must not be allowed to become so infatuated with their schemes that they neglect recovery techniques.

TWO CATEGORIES   There are two types of data damage. In one a few data
OF DATA DAMAGE   items or records may be harmed; they can be corrected
relatively quickly provided that there is some means of knowing what the correct records should be. In the other, an entire data base is destroyed or a large segment of it; the damage is too extensive to be corrected by manual methods. One hopes that the latter massive damage will never occur. However, it would be folly to assume that it cannot. A reconstruction program must be in existence to deal with the eventuality of massive data-base damage.

Data can be made reconstructable by copying them periodically onto tape, and copying those transactions which change them. These copies are stored securely, away from the computer center.

PROFESSIONAL   Details of security safeguards are beyond the scope of
APPROACH   this short book. They can be read elsewhere (19).
Let us stress that a professional approach is needed in designing and implementing the safeguards. Often, tight security is found only in a centralized installation, not in small peripheral installations. Only a portion of an organization's data, however, needs **tight** security. Data which form a basis for embezzlement need tight security; data such as customer addresses do not.

The end user can be assured that if good professional security measures are used, no **unauthorized** person is likely to read or tamper with his data. He might, however, be concerned with who is **authorized.**

10 CONSIDERATIONS WHICH AFFECT MACHINE PERFORMANCE

INTRODUCTION   The end user is not involved in the design of the **physical** data structures nor in general with design that affects machine performance. This is complex and is handled by a data-base expert. These are, however, certain factors about machine performance that users should understand.

DATA-BASE QUERIES   Data-base queries can be classified into four types.

1. **Primary-key queries.** A record is accessed by means of its primary key. This can be done quickly and uses few machine cycles.

An example of a primary-key query would be "PRINT DETAILS OF THE SHIP ACHILLES." SHIP-NAME is a primary key for accessing a naval data base. A single record is looked up, and its contents are printed.

2. **Single-secondary-key queries.** This type of query may be represented on a data model diagram as a secondary-key path. If it is anticipated a secondary index or other mechanism may be used. It requires far more machine cycles than does a primary-key query.

An example of a single-secondary-key query would be "PRINT DETAILS OF ALL SHIPS WITH A READINESS-RATING = C1." If the question was anticipated by the system designer there may be a secondary-key index showing what ships have a given readiness rating.

3. **Multiple-secondary-key queries.** This requires more than one secondary-key access. It can be substantially more complex and expensive in machine cycles than a single-secondary-key access.

An example of such a query might be "PRINT DETAILS OF ALL RUSSIAN SHIPS WITHIN 900 MILES OF THE STRAITS OF HORMUZ CARRYING TORPEDOES WITH A RANGE GREATER THAN 20 MILES." A secondary index to the weapons data base may be used to find which weapons are torpedoes with a range greater than 20 miles. There may be a secondary-key index showing which ships are Russian. It may be necessary to examine their records to find whether they carry those weapons. This produces a list of ships. The area around the Straits of Hormuz is then examined to find which ships are within 900 miles of that location. These ships are compared with the previous list. This requires a considerable amount of machine activity, especially if there are many ships.

4. **Unanticipated search queries.** Secondary-key queries may take place relatively quickly if there is a suitable secondary index. If there is not, then it may be necessary to search the records in question a record at a time. This is very expensive in machine time.

DEDICATED MACHINES   If a computer did nothing other than process one query at a time, a relatively inexpensive machine might be used. Even if it processed multiple similar queries at once, machine time need not be a serious problem.

Unfortunately, many systems are designed to do conventional high-volume data processing, with queries fitting in as required. A DP manager has to decide which activities have priority. Queries about Russian ships near the Straits of Hormuz may have very high priority, but ordinary commercial use of an end-user query language may not.

The end user with a language like QUERY-BY-EXAMPLE can very quickly enter a query like the following:

EMPLOYEE	EMPLOYEE#	NAME	LOCATION	SALARY	YEAR-OF-HIRE
	A	P.	P.	< 25000	>1975

SKILLS	SKILL-TYPE	GRADE	EMPLOYEE#
	ACCOUNTANT	>6	A

The user may have no concept of how much is involved in processing this query. The response time might be quite long. If this type of query is given a low priority, the response time might become degraded to a level which seems unacceptable to end users. If the necessary secondary indices do not exist and the EMPLOYEE or SKILLS records have to be searched, the time taken may be excessive.

EXPENSE   When a query initiates the searching of a data base on a large system, it may be more expensive than the end user realizes. Often there is no indication of the cost involved when a data-base facility is used. The user may not know the wide difference in cost between a primary-key query and one which triggers searching operations. It would be useful if computers would tell the user the cost before they process the query, but most do not.

Sometimes user management is surprised by the charges and unable to comprehend them.

CATEGORIES OF
DATA SYSTEMS

Figure 10.1 shows six categories of data systems. In its early years data-base usage employed predominently primary-key access paths. The high volume activity of most computers is category 1 in Fig. 10.1: production data processing. Primary-key queries are used with the production systems with no problem (category 2).

Off-line secondary-key queries can be saved and processed in a scheduled batch fashion (category 3 in Fig. 10.1). This does not disrupt the production system.

Category 4 is much more disruptive of the production system. A data base designed to be efficient for high-volume production is not usually efficient for complex secondary-key queries, and vice versa. Category 6 is worse. The queries are not planned and may require parts of the data base to be searched.

It is often desirable that categories 4 and 6 be in a separate computer system to the category 1 high-volume production systems. End-user departments might have their own computer—either an information system or a production system.

| | IS THE INFORMATION PRODUCED ON A SCHEDULED BASIS BY THE SYSTEM? | |
	YES SCHEDULED	NO ON–DEMAND
PRIMARY – KEY	① PRODUCTION DATA PROCESSING	② SIMPLE QUERIES
ANTICIPATED SINGLE–SECONDARY–KEY AND MULTIPLE–SECONDARY–KEY	③ COMPLEX OFF–LINE QUERIES	④ COMPLEX ON–LINE QUERIES
UNANTICIPATED	⑤ SLOW–REACTION INFORMATION SYSTEM	⑥ GENERALIZED INFORMATION SYSTEM

Figure 10.1 Categories of data systems. Categories 4 and 6 may need to be in a different computer from category 1.

This may make sense both for performance and other reasons. It is discussed in Chapter 11.

Category 5 in Fig. 10.1 is less useful. Nonpredefined information requests might be satisfied by visual inspections of listings produced on a scheduled basis. Although this has been common with some computer systems, it is generally a rather unsatisfactory way of answering spontaneous requests for information.

**PHYSICAL
DATA-BASE
DESIGN**   A data model showing logical associations, such as that in Fig. 6.3, does not contain enough information to perform efficient **physical**-data-base design. To do this the data-base designer needs three more pieces of information:

1. For each double-head arrow showing a one-to-many association it is necessary to know **how many.** In the case

how many B data items are associated on average with one A data item?

This number can be coded in the input views of data that are used. It may be written against each double-head arrow. Thus,

means that an invoice has 5 items on it, on average.

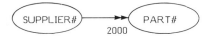

means that a supplier supplies 2000 parts on average, although one particular supplier may at one time supply 0, 1, or many parts.

2. For each of the usage paths represented in the model (each line between bubbles) it is desirable to know *how often it is followed.*

When individual user views are created, the number of times per month each view is employed can be stated. The synthesis process adds up the usage of each path as it builds the data model. DATA DESIGNER, for example, prints these usage path figures in its output reports ready for the physical data-base designer.

3. Similarly, for each usage path it is desirable to know whether it is followed with **on-line** processing or **batch** processing. If **on-line,** is a fast response time required?

SCHEDULING AND RESPONSE-TIME PROBLEMS

Some data-base systems have severe scheduling and response-time problems. This is especially so when secondary-key paths have high-volume usage. DP operations are tending to swing from mainly primary-key usage of data to a substantial amount of secondary-key usage. This will be increasingly so in the future as good end-user data-base inquiry languages become popular.

Figure 6.3 shows the key paths. A large traffic figure associated with a secondary-key path is an indication of potential scheduling problems.

Given the falling cost of minicomputer information systems, it often makes sense to create functional information systems **separate** from the high-volume production systems. The secondary-key paths in the data model may indicate a need for this. Chapter 11 discusses the use of separate end-user data bases.

The physical-data-base designer needs to work closely with the data administrator (if it is not the same person). For performance reasons the physical-data-base designer might decide to split the model into separate data bases, or to make minor deviations from the model structure. Such decisions should be discussed with the data administrator and their effect on future user requirements examined.

Whereas the primary-key linkages on Fig. 6.3 are often predictable in their usage, secondary-key usage may grow suddenly and unpredictably, especially as powerful end-user languages spread. The data administrator may use the models and discussion of them with end-user groups to predict the forms of secondary-key usage and be ready for them.

11 SEPARATE END-USER SYSTEMS

Some computers and storage are continuing to drop in cost so that it is economical for end-user departments to have their own computer and store their own data.

CENTRALIZATION VS. DECENTRALIZATION   It is desirable to look at the properties of data which lead naturally to local storage, or conversely to centralized storage. These are listed in Box 11.1. Even if the cost of storage dropped to zero there would be certain data which, by their nature, ought to be stored centrally. For example, data which are being continually updated from many locations ought to be maintained at **one** location. This is done with reservation systems for airlines, hotels, and rented cars. It is done on inventory control systems, military early warning systems, and so on.

The sharing of data among multiple applications tends to lead to centralized data-base facilities. Increasingly, a large organization does not have one center of activity, but many. The computers in different factories and different offices are interconnected and may share data in a distributed fashion. Distributed data-base systems are coming into existence.

The pattern of usage and updates may determine whether data are centralized or dispersed. Figure 11.1 illustrates how different patterns lead to different placing of data. This is discussed more fully in Reference 20.

USERS KEEPING THEIR OWN DATA   Often, end users want to keep their own data for a variety of reasons.

First, they feel that they own the data and can maintain privacy. Nobody else can interfere with their data. As we stressed in Chapter 9, the data can be equally private and more secure in a centralized data base (with professional security).

121

USERS

		USERS ARE IN ONE LOCATION		USERS ARE GEOGRAPHICALLY DISPERSED	
		UP-TO-THE-SECOND INFORMATION REQUIRED	INFORMATION PROVIDED CAN BE HOURS OLD	UP-TO-THE-SECOND INFORMATION REQUIRED	INFORMATION PROVIDED CAN BE HOURS OLD
INFREQUENT UPDATES	UPDATES FROM ONE SOURCE	ONE LOCATION		DATA CAN BE DISPERSED WITH UPDATES DISTRIBUTED VIA A NETWORK	
	UPDATES FROM GEOGRAPHICALLY DISPERSED SOURCES	DATA ARE CENTRALIZED AT THE LOCATION OF THE USERS		DATA ARE CENTRALIZED, OR DISPERSED, WITH UPDATES DISTRIBUTED VIA A NETWORK	DATA CAN BE DISPERSED WITH UPDATES DISTRIBUTED BY BATCH TRANSMISSION
FREQUENT UPDATES	UPDATES FROM ONE SOURCE	ONE LOCATION			
	UPDATES FROM GEOGRAPHICALLY DISPERSED SOURCES	DATA ARE CENTRALIZED AT THE LOCATION OF THE USERS		DATA ARE CENTRALIZED	DATA ARE CENTRALIZED, OR DISPERSED, WITH UPDATES DISTRIBUTED BY BATCH TRANSMISSION

UPDATES

Figure 11.1 The pattern of usage and updates may determine whether data are centralized or dispersed. A high rate of updates from dispersed sources and differently dispersed users needing up-to-the-second data is an argument for centralization.

Second, they are independent of the scheduling and availability problems of the DP center.

Third, they are free to develop their own applications. Often this is important because the DP center has a large application backlog and is reluctant to take on more work.

Fourth, they can use a level of imagination and inventiveness in application development which may be lacking in the DP department. The end users understand the subtleties of their own applications and can sometimes apply a high creativity in devising the facilities they need to do a better job.

USER INITIATIVE   On the whole the best thing that could happen in computing is for end users everywhere to take the initiative in divising their own systems. However, it needs to be done in such a way that it does not harm the use of data elsewhere in the organization.

BOX 11.1   Centralization and decentralization of data

**Properties inherent in certain data which lead
naturally to decentralization**

1. The data are used at one peripheral location; they are rarely or never used at other locations. To transmit such data for storage may be unnecessarily complex and expensive.

2. The accuracy, privacy, and security of the data are a local responsibility.

3. The files are simple and are used by one or a few applications. Hence, there would be little or no advantage in employing data-base software.

4. The update rate is too high for a single centralized storage system.

5. Peripheral files are searched or manipulated with an end-user language which implicitly results in inverted list or secondary-key operations. Too many end-user operations of this type can play havoc with the performance of a central system. They may be better located in a peripheral system with end users responsible for their usage and costs.

**Properties inherent in certain data which lead
naturally to centralization**

1. Data are used by centralized applications such as a corporate-wide payroll, purchasing, or general accounting.

2. Users in all areas need access to the same data and need the current up-to-the-minute version. The data are frequently updated. Data may be centralized to avoid the problems of real-time synchronization of multiple copies with a high update level.

3. Users of the data travel among many separate locations, and it is cheaper to centralize their data than to provide a switched data network.

4. The data as a whole will be searched. They are part of an **information system** which will provide answers to spontaneous queries from users, many of which can only be answered by examining many records. Searching data which are geographically scattered is extremely time consuming. The software and hardware for efficient searching re-

Continued

BOX 11.1 *Continued*

quire the data to be in one location. Secondary indices may be used and the indexing software refers only to data in one storage system.

5. A high level of security is to be maintained over the data. The protection procedures may be expensive, possibly involving a well-guarded, secure vault, and tight control of authorized users. The data are better guarded if they are in one location, with external backup copies, than if they are scattered. Catastrophe protection is often an argument for bicentral systems rather than for single centralized storage.

6. The data are too bulky to be stored on inexpensive peripheral storage units. The economies of scale of centralized bulk storage are desirable.

7. To make systems auditable, details are sometimes kept of what transactions updated certain data. It may be cheaper, and more secure, to dump these in a large centralized archival storage unit.

Some end-user installations employ data which are not used anywhere else in the corporation. But these are exceptional. Most end users employ some data which are of value elsewhere. They use data from other data bases and create data which will be employed in other areas. Much transmission of data occurs between end-user computers and data systems elsewhere in the organization.

In such an environment it is vital that the data items have the same definition and the same bit representation in different installations. When data are passed between a user system and a data-base installation they should be compatible with that data base. The data structures employed in the user systems should be treated as views of data which are included in the overall data modeling process. The record structures which result from the modeling should be used in the peripheral installations.

In other words, the work of the data administrator needs to be distributed. The data dictionary and the data modeling process should apply to all data in all computers in the organization (with a few exceptions such as laboratory work, where the data may be genuinely unique to that location).

This is often not the case. End-user departments in many organizations have implemented minicomputer files without regard to the data needs elsewhere in the corporation. Their programmers see only the needs of their own department, and create their own data items with their own bit structure. End users need to understand that this is harmful. The data so created cannot be used elsewhere without expensive conversion. Sometimes no conversion is possible because the data items are defined differently. Furthermore, the programmers fail to extract data that would be useful from data bases elsewhere.

The end result of totally uncontrolled application development by users is data chaos, with the same data being represented in all manner of different ways in different departments.

The data administrator should help the end users in setting up their own data resources, and he needs their cooperation.

One of the most critical decisions in the planning of data processing is what activities should be centralized and what decentralized (21). What should be done in a central DP department and what in end-user departments? A valuable pattern that is emerging is some end users exhibiting a high level of initiative and creativity in establishing their own systems, but this within a controlled framework which is centrally established. A good DP department should help end users to establish facilities, when they want to, which fit into the corporate networks and corporate data modeling.

SEPARATE DATA ENTRY

Many corporations have moved the data-entry process from centralized keypunching areas to the end-user departments. The end users are made responsible for the entry of their own data, and for its accuracy. When mistakes are found, they must correct them.

This change has resulted in a major improvement in the accuracy of the data. When users are responsible for their own data, they are more careful.

The data being entered may reside in end-user computers or remote, shared computers. Either way, it needs to be incorporated in the overall modeling process.

MINICOMPUTER DATA BASES

In the early days of end user minicomputers, these machines kept **files** not **data bases.** Data bases originally needed the software of large computers. Now data-base management is becoming available on small computers. (Caution is needed because some minicomputer vendors who do not have a data-base management system falsely refer in their sales literature to their on-line **file** storage capability as **data base.**)

When end-user **file** records are designed, these records should be one of the user views in the overall modeling process. The data administrator should advise the users about the grouping of data items into records. When end-user **data bases** are used, these and the central data bases should be designed with a common modeling process.

Various problems with accuracy and conformity of updating can occur when replicated data exists at more than one location. The data administrator should establish the rules that avoid these problems (20).

PROBLEMS OF   What has often happened in practice is that a central-
RAPID GROWTH   ized service has been introduced for end users which is
                           suddenly perceived by them to be very useful. They
then increase their utilization of service until the load on the central computer
becomes excessive. The service then appears to degrade, giving much longer
response times and sometimes being unavailable due to scheduling problems. This
degradation of a service that was good is very frustrating and the users tend to be
critical of the DP department.

A somewhat cynical law of complex computer systems (Martin's Law) says:
"If a service is created which is sufficiently useful, utilization will expand until it
knocks out the system!"

There are countless examples of systems following the type of growth pattern
in Fig. 11.2. Growth is slow at first because end users are reluctant to change their

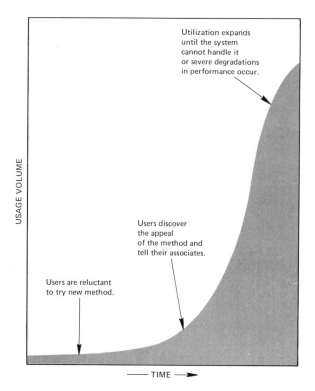

Figure 11.2   Martin's Law: "If a service is created which is sufficiently useful, utilization will expand until it knocks out the system!" Many end-user services have had a growth pattern similar to this diagram.

methods of working. A few end users discover the value of the new methods and tell their friends. The good news spreads and the utilization expands far beyond that anticipated by the designers.

In the 1970s most data were accessed by means of a **primary key** such as CUSTOMER NUMBER, JOB NUMBER, PASSENGER NAME and FLIGHT NUMBER, and so on. Increasingly, **secondary keys** came into use so that data could be accessed by more than one key. For example jobs could be accessed by specifying which customer they were for, as well as by JOB NUMBER. Data bases could be queried to obtain information such as "List all surgical patients under 30 in the last year who have gone into coma."

The more we employ higher-level data-base languages, the more secondary-key operations, as opposed to primary-key operations, will be initiated.

We stressed in Chapter 10 that this can give performance problems. Response time on some systems is poor for queries involving secondary-key actions. Response time, and often availability of systems as perceived by the terminal user, is affected by the job scheduling. Where many different types of activities take place on the same machine, scheduling becomes complex. Changes in schedules are made frequently and these sometimes affect the end user adversely. With complex queries (and sometimes less complex ones) he can perceive a sudden drop in response time from 3 seconds, say, to 30 seconds or sometimes much longer. This is extremely frustrating for the user.

This is a problem both with large computers and minicomputers. The terminal-user response time on a minicomputer can suddenly go to pieces when the machine is doing compilations, sorts, and so on.

Conversely, the data-processing manager is often concerned that much high-level data-base query usage will play havoc with the performance of the system's other activities.

This is a problem of too much complexity in a single machine. The solution is to remove some of the activity into separate cheap machines. In particular the data structures for a high level of secondary-key usage should usually not be mixed up with the data structures for production runs.

SEPARATE INFORMATION SYSTEMS

Because of the general incompatibility of high-volume production runs and complex information system activity, it often pays to separate the information system from the production system. In some cases a minicomputer information system has been installed to provide certain types of users with specific information.

Although it may contain much of the same data, the information system should often be separate from the production system and use a separate collection of data. The reasons for the two collections of data being separate and disjoint are as follows:

1. The physical data structures used for information systems are such that it is difficult or excessively time-consuming to keep the data up to date. Production systems, on the other hand, have simpler data structures which can be designed for fast updating.

2. More serious, it is very difficult to insert new data and delete old data from the information system data base except by lengthy off-line operations. Production systems have data structures into which records can easily be inserted or deleted.

3. Production systems usually have to contain the latest transactions. However, it usually does not matter if an information system gives information which is 24 hours or more out of date.

4. Production systems may handle a high throughput of transactions so that file structures permitting rapid access are necessary to cope with the volume. Information systems containing the same data usually handle a relatively small number of queries.

5. The information system may contain summary information or digested information without all the details that are in the production system.

6. End users employing an information system may want freedom from the constraints placed on machine usage by the management of a high-volume production-oriented system.

7. Powerful languages for end-use information systems are becoming available, but management of the production system do not want end users to have free access to the production data with these languages. They prefer the end users to have their own files where they can do no harm.

8. Job scheduling is complex on systems handling widely different types of transactions and jobs. Changes in the scheduling or in the job mix can play havoc with response times. A flood of queries using secondary-key operations will interfere with the production runs and their deadlines.

9. DP managers responsible for production runs are reluctant to give end users too much freedom to use high-level data-base languages because they may adversely affect performance or even damage the data.

10. End users need their own information systems to tune and adjust, to meet their own varying information needs. They should keep their own data in their own information systems.

The production system is updated in real time. Often there is on-line data entry at end-user locations. The information system is updated off-line, possibly each night, with files prepared by the production system. The production system files may have a high ratio of new records being inserted and old ones deleted, but this volatility can be reasonably easily accommodated. The information system is not concerned with real-time insertions and deletions because new records are inserted off-line.

Figure 11.3 illustrates this approach. The system on the left might, for example, be a sales order entry system with terminals in branch sales offices. Its files are updated in real time, and many modifications to the data have to be made in real time. New items must be inserted into the files as they arise. The files are all struc-

PRODUCTION SYSTEM

- Complete data.

- Updated continuously.

- Data accessed
  by primary keys.

- Simple primary-key inquiries.

- Insertions and deletions are
  straightforward but must be
  handled in real time.

- Complex operating system.

- Often on-line data entry.

- High volume of transactions.

- Complex scheduling of work.

- Main design criterion: **EFFICIENCY OF HIGH-
  VOLUME PROCESSING.**

INFORMATION SYSTEM

- Summary data.

- Updated periodically.

- Data structured so that
  they can be searched using
  multiple secondary keys.

- Psychologically powerful
  end-user language.

- Insertions and deletions are
  complex because of the secondary
  keys, but are handled off-line in
  periodic nightly maintenance runs.

- Simple control program.

- Off-line updates.

- Low volume of transactions.

- Scheduling problems avoided.

- Main design criterion: **EASE OF USE AND VALUE
  TO END USERS.**

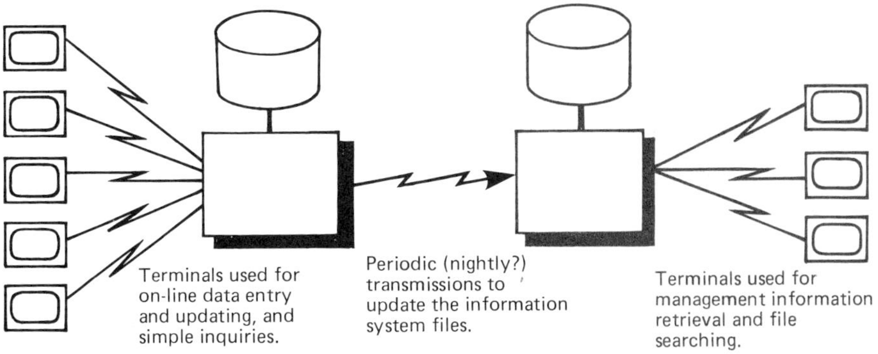

Terminals used for
on-line data entry
and updating, and
simple inquiries.

Periodic (nightly?)
transmissions to
update the information
system files.

Terminals used for
management information
retrieval and file
searching.

Figure 11.3 Information systems should often be separate from production systems even though they contain much of the same data because the
characteristics of their data structure and usage are fundamentally different.

tured and manipulated on the basis of primary keys such as PART-NUMBER and
CUSTOMER-NUMBER. Although the files are volatile, a fairly straightforward
technique can be devised for handling insertions and deletions.

The system on the right on Fig. 11.3 is designed to provide information to end
users. It provides powerful end-user query languages. End users may also keep and
modify their own files in it. To answer a diverse set of such queries spontaneously,
the system uses special index or pointer structures. Inserting new records with these

structures is complicated and time-consuming because the secondary indices or pointer structures must be updated. It is therefore done off-line when the terminals are not in use. The data for the off-line updating is transmitted by the system on the left-hand side of Fig. 11.3. If this technique were not used, the volatility would be very difficult to handle.

The production system handles a high volume of transactions. A major design criterion is to maximize the efficiency of high-volume processing. Data and system structures are selected with this objective. The information system handles a very low volume of transactions compared to the production system. The design criterion is therefore not to optimize machine efficiency but to optimize the ease of use and value to the end users.

Until the late 1970s information systems tended to be centralized systems. As minicomputers became more powerful it became practical to have information systems in user departments, sometimes with very small computers.

In many cases the data stored in the information system occupy much less storage than those in the production system—they are only summary data. Therefore, a small minicomputer is appropriate. In other cases the information system storage must be very large because historical or archival data are kept.

There will be inquiries into the production system as well as the information system, but they will be mostly **primary-key** inquiries, often requesting a degree of detail that does not exist in the information system. It may be desirable that the end-user terminal connected to the information system is also linked to the production system of Fig. 11.3, or possibly to many production systems, so that managers or users can inspect detailed records of customers, bank statements, orders, and so on, when they need to.

The production system has a complex operating system, and the scheduling of jobs on it is complex. The information system may have a simple operating system or control program which handles the low volume of queries in a first-come-first-served fashion.

The main design concern with the production system is **efficiency** of high-volume operations. With the information system there is little concern with machine efficiency. The main design concerns are **effectiveness, ease of use,** and **value to end users.**

Get involved

Whatever configurations are finally used, one aspect of data processing is clear. We are leaving the age when end users could be treated as knowing nothing about it. With today's systems it is becoming increasingly important that users understand the potentials of computing in their jobs, and **become involved.**

THE PROCEDURE FOR CANONICAL DATA-BASE DESIGN

1. Take the first user's view of data and draw it in the form of a bubble chart—a graph with point-to-point directed links between single data items, representing associations of the two types: 1 and M.

Where a concatenated key is used, draw this as one bubble, and draw the component data items of the concatenated key as separate bubbles, thus:

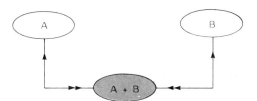

Check that the representation avoids hidden transitive dependencies. Where a concatenated key data item has to be used, ensure that all single-arrow links from it go to data items which are dependent on the full concatenated key, not merely part of it. In other words, ensure that the representation of the user's view is in third normal form.

Otherwise, draw only the associations which concern this user.

2. Take the next user's view, representing it as above. Merge it into the graph. Check for any synonyms or homonyms, removing them if they appear.

3. In the resulting graph distinguish between the attribute nodes and the primary-key nodes. (A primary-key node has one or more single-arrow links leaving it.) Mark the primary keys in some way, for example, in red.

4. For each association between keys, add the inverse association if it is not already on the graph. If this results in an M:M link between keys, determine whether the inverse association would ever be used in reality. If it could be used at any time in the future, replace it by introducing an extra concatenated key incorporating the key data items that were linked.

5. Examine the associations and identify any that appear redundant. For any associations that are candidates for removal, check carefully that their meaning is genuinely redundant; if so, remove them.

6.   Repeat the previous four steps until all user views are merged into the graph.

7.   Identify the root keys. (A root key is a primary key with no single arrow leaving it to another key.)

For pictorial clarity the diagram should be rearranged with the root keys at the top. The single-arrow links between keys should point upward where possible. The links between primary keys may be marked in color.

8.   Observe whether the graph contains any isolated attributes. An isolated attribute is a node with no single-arrow links entering or leaving it (only double-arrow links). An isolated attribute could be treated in one of three ways:

(a)   It may be implemented as a repeating attribute in a variable-length record.
(b)   It may be treated as a solitary key—a one-data-item record.
(c)   It may be the result of an error in interpretation of the user's data, in which case the error is corrected.

9.   Adjust the graph to avoid any intersecting attributes. (An intersecting attribute is an attribute with more than one single-arrow link entering it.) An intersecting attribute can be avoided by:

(a)   Replacing one or more links to it with equivalent links via an existing key.
(b)   Duplicating the data item in question.
(c)   Treating it as a solitary key—a one-data-item record.

10.   Redraw the data items arranged into groups (records, segments, tuples), each having one primary key and its associated attributes. A group may now be drawn as a box.

11.   Identify all secondary keys. (A secondary key is an attribute with one or more double-arrow links leaving it.) Draw the secondary-key links between the boxes.

12.   The unconstrained "canonical" schema may now be converted into the more constrained view associated with a particular software package. It is generally a simple step to convert the canonical schema into a CODASYL, DL/I, or relational schema. Some software, however, has constraints that would require a major deviation from, or splitting of, the canonical view. Some software will simply not be able to handle it.

In converting the canonical schema to a particular software schema, performance considerations associated with high-usage and fast-response paths should be examined. We suggest the following steps:

(a)   Mark all paths which are used in interactive systems and which need fast response time.
(b)   Estimate the number of times per month each user path will be traversed. Add up how often each association will be traversed (in each direction when applicable).
(c)   Estimate the length of each group.
(d)   For each M association, estimate the size of M, that is, how many values on average are associated with one value, or how many "child" groups are associated with a "parent" group.

The information above may affect the choice of structure and may cause the designer to modify the schema. In some cases a group may be split because it contains a mixture of frequently used and rarely used data, or is too long. In some cases a schema will be split to avoid complexity.

13.   With the software schema designed, return to the original user views and ensure that they can be handled by it. In some cases the performance cost of handling a particular user view is sufficiently great that it is worthwhile to completely modify that user view.

|| CLASS QUESTIONS

Chapter 1—What Is a Data Base?

1. Define and state the objectives of a data base.

2. Discuss the need for involvement of end users with a data base.

3. What do you understand by the term "end user"?

4. Describe the methods and problems that existed before the advent of computers.

5. Discuss why data are valuable in a corporation or organization.

6. Describe the tasks that a corporation or organization needs to define when looking at data to be employed in a data base.

Chapter 2—Productivity and Flexibility

1. Describe the main problems that management faces with information from existing computer systems.

2. Describe briefly the problems experienced with file systems.

3. Why is maintenance normally avoided in a data base?

4. Define a data-base management system.

5. Describe why data independence is important in a data base.

6. Specify methods by which ad hoc requests can be met in a data base.

7. Describe briefly why constant change in data processing has to be planned for.

8. More than one data base may exist in a corporation or organization. Discuss this statement and give reasons why this would occur.

Chapter 3—Who Does What?

1. Describe the differences and effects of data-base operation and file operation.

2. Give examples of how data items can be used in multiple records.

3. Give examples of how data base may be shared by multiple organizations.

4. Describe why data definition and modeling are important in a data base.

5. Define a data administrator.

6. Specify the best procedure for setting up a data base.

7. Define a data-base designer and describe the difference between a data-base designer and a data administrator.

8. Describe the steps in the design process of a data base.

9. Describe why the end-user group is important to the success of a data base.

10. Describe the differences between subject data base and application data base. Give examples.

11. What is a data strategist, and how does this position fit into a corporation or organization? Compare this with the data administrator.

12. Describe what is meant by production systems and information systems.

Chapter 4—What Are Data?

1. Define a data item. What is its alternative name?

2. Describe why it is necessary for data to be defined, cataloged, and organized.

3. Give examples of the following values of data items in bubble chart form.
    3.1. One to one   3.2. One to zero, one, or many

4. In terms of a bubble chart, define the following:
    4.1. Primary key   4.2. Secondary key
    4.3. Attribute

Chapter 5—Data Modeling

1. Discuss why data modeling and the organization of logical structure are so important.

2. Why is maintenance a problem in existing programs?

3. Define the tasks and responsibilities of a data administrator.

4. Describe the role of the end users in data modeling.

5. Define the methods by which a data administrator may effectively design a data base.

6. Clear presentation of designs is important. Discuss this statement.

7. Describe briefly the data synthesis of data modeling.

8. Draw bubble charts for the following data items and show their relationships.

    * Teacher   * Classroom   * Headmaster

    * Pupil   * Lesson

Chapter 6—Design Tools for End Users

1. Give examples of design tools important to end users.

2. What do you understand by the term "data dictionary"?

3. List the advantages of using a data dictionary and give examples of its function.

4. Describe the function of a data modeling tool.

5. Define the problems that arise when there is pressure brought to bear on the application development process. What can be done to overcome these problems?

Chapter 7—How to Succeed with Data Modeling

1. State the objectives of data modeling and define the stability of the design.

2. Describe the questions individuals in a corporation or organization should ask when thinking about the future of data.

3. Complexity of user views might be a problem. Discuss this statement and draw a conclusion.

4. Describe the conversion process from file systems to data base. What is the most significant factor?

5. Define the steps to success when using data modeling techniques.

6. Draw a bubble chart for the following data items and show their relationships.

    • Zoo   • Animal   • Keeper
    • Cage

Chapter 8—Data-Base Language for End Users

1. State as many rules as you can for the programmed end-user dialogues.

2. Describe the differences between off-line and on-line query languages.

3. Discuss query languages in terms of spontaneity and state the advantages.

4. Describe at least three capabilities of a powerful data-base language.

5. Give an example of a forms-oriented language.

6. State some of the advantages of QUERY-BY-EXAMPLE.

7. Describe a specimen of QUERY-BY-EXAMPLE using the "Print" feature, using the following query.

Display all the SALARIES of all employees.

8. QUERY-BY-EXAMPLE can update data as well. Give an example.

9. Give an example of how QUERY-BY-EXAMPLE uses data that are invented or skeleton in nature.

10. State some of the logical operators that can be used with QUERY-BY-EXAMPLE.

11. More than one table can be utilized with QUERY-BY-EXAMPLE. State some of the benefits of this.

12. Describe as many of the functions of QUERY-BY-EXAMPLE as you can.

13. What do you understand by the term "condition box"?

14. Compare COBOL to QUERY-BY-EXAMPLE and discuss the differences. State which you feel is more efficient and give your reasons.

Chapter 9—Ownership of Data, and Privacy

1. State at least three of the questions that users should ask themselves regarding the ownership of data.

2. Describe the most important aspects of security design.

3. Discuss the differences between the custodian of data and the owner of data.

4. Describe some of the methods that can make data secure.

5. What are the dangers when the use of powerful high-level languages are employed?

6. Give definitions of the following:

   6.1. Data security   6.2. Privacy

7. List at least four of the essentials of data-base security.

8. Describe one type of data-base security exposure for each of the following:

   8.1. Acts of God   8.2. Mechanical failure
   8.3. Human carelessness   8.4. Malicious damage
   8.5. Crime   8.6. Invasion of privacy

9. Describe briefly the three ways in which security exposure can be minimized.

10. Discuss some of the design aspects of security safeguards.

Chapter 10—Considerations Which Affect Machine Performance

1. Define primary-key queries.

2. Give an example of a multiple-secondary-key query.

3. Describe why unanticipated search queries are expensive in machine time.

4. Expense can be a problem when searching a data base. Discuss this statement and suggest a possible solution.

5. Describe why complex on-line queries can be disruptive in a production system.

6. Scheduling and response times are important aspects which affect machine performance. Give examples to illustrate this statement.

Chapter 11—Separate End-User Systems

1. Describe at least three of the differences between centralization versus decentralization of data.

2. State examples of systems that have
   2.1. Centralized data   2.2. Decentralized data

3. State the reasons why users prefer to keep their own data.

4. Discuss the important aspects of users who take the initiative in devising their own systems.

5. What are the advantages to users who allow decentralized data entry?

6. Describe at least three reasons why information systems should be separate from production systems.

REFERENCES

1. R. L. Nolan, Computer Data Bases: The Future Is Now, *Harvard Business Review,* Sept.–Oct. 1973.

2. Ibid. (The rest of Mr. Nolan's article is excellent!)

3. From a systems study for the state of Arkansas prepared by the Information Systems Planning Staff of the Office of the Information Systems Executive Committee, State of Arkansas, 1974.

4. From an internal IBM description of its Common Manufacturing Information System.

5. E. F. Codd, Further Normalization of the Data Base Relational Model: in *Courant Computer Science Symposia,* Vol. 6, Prentice-Hall, Inc., Englewood Cliffs, N.J., 1272.

6. J. Martin, *Computer Data Base Organization,* 2nd ed., Prentice-Hall, Inc., Englewood Cliffs, N.J., 1977, Chap. 14.

7. DATA MANAGER manuals, available from Management Systems and Programming Ltd., MSP Inc, 21 Worthen Road, Lexington, Mass. 02173

8. *How to Do Optimal Logical Data Base Design,* a manual on DATA DESIGNER, available from the DMW Group, 2395 Huron Parkway, Ann Arbor, Michigan 48104.

9. Manuals and information on the MARK IV File Management System are available from Informatics Inc., MARK IV Systems Company, 21050 Vanowen St., Canoga Park, California 91303.

10. GIS manuals are available from IBM Corp., 1133 Westchester Ave., White Plains, New York 10604.

11. This example is taken from an IBM slide presentation on GIS/VS, No. GV 20–0480, Nov. 1973.

12. D. D. Chamberlain et al., SEQUEL 2: A Unified Approach to Data Definition, Manipulation and Control. *IBM Journal of Research and Development*, Vol. 20, pp. 560–575, 1976.

13. G. D. Held, M. R. Stonebraker, and E. Wong, INGERS: A Relational Data Base System, *Proc. National Computer Conference*, Vol. 44, 1975.

14. NOMAD is a language for application development using data bases on the NCSS time-sharing network. National CSS, Inc., 187 Danbury Road, Wilton, Connecticut 06897.

15. M. M. Zloof, QUERY-BY-EXAMPLE: A Data Base Language, *IBM Systems Journal,* No. 4, 1977.

16. J. C. Thomas and J. D. Gould, A Psychological Study of QUERY-BY-EXAMPLE, *Proc. National Computer Conference,* Vol. 44, pp. 439–445, 1975.

17. M. M. Zloof, *QUERY-BY-EXAMPLE: A Data-Base Management Language,* IBM Research Report available from the author, IBM Thomas J. Watson Research Center, Yorktown Heights, New York 10598.

18. The COBOL program is reproduced from D. Kapp and J. F. Leben, *IMS Programming Techniques,* Van Nostrand Reinhold, New York, 1978. This reference contains more details of the program and data base used.

19. J. Martin, *Security, Accuracy, and Privacy in Computer Systems,* Prentice-Hall, Inc., Englewood Cliffs, N.J., 1973.

20. J. Martin, *Distributed File and Data-Base Design: Tools and Techniques,* Savant Research Studies, 2 New Street, Carnforth, Lancs, LA5 9BX England, 1979.

21. J. Martin, *Corporate Strategy for Distributed Data Processing,* Savant Research Studies, Carnforth, Lancs, LA5 9BX England, 1979.

INDEX

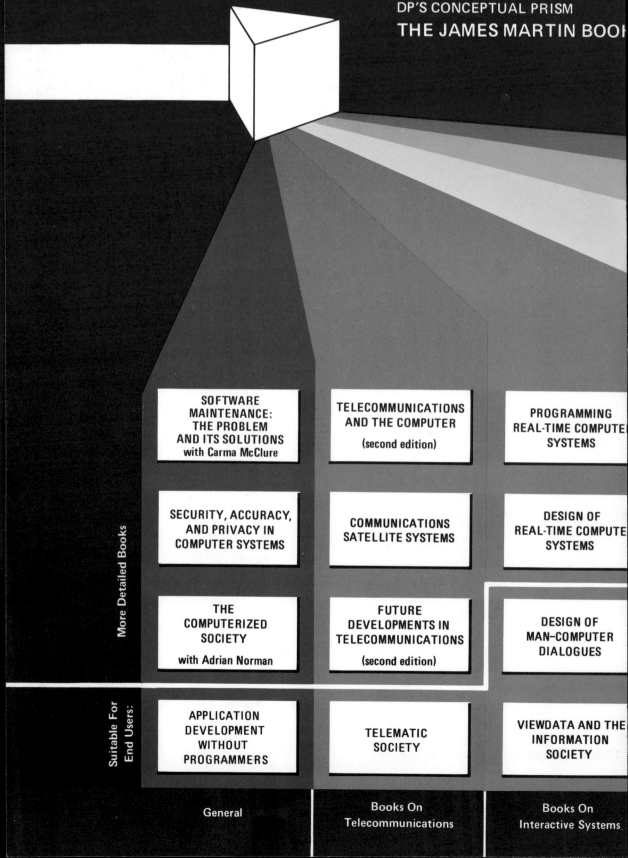

DP'S CONCEPTUAL PRISM

THE JAMES MARTIN BOOK

More Detailed Books

Suitable For End Users:

General	Books On Telecommunications	Books On Interactive Systems
SOFTWARE MAINTENANCE: THE PROBLEM AND ITS SOLUTIONS with Carma McClure	TELECOMMUNICATIONS AND THE COMPUTER (second edition)	PROGRAMMING REAL-TIME COMPUTER SYSTEMS
SECURITY, ACCURACY, AND PRIVACY IN COMPUTER SYSTEMS	COMMUNICATIONS SATELLITE SYSTEMS	DESIGN OF REAL-TIME COMPUTER SYSTEMS
THE COMPUTERIZED SOCIETY with Adrian Norman	FUTURE DEVELOPMENTS IN TELECOMMUNICATIONS (second edition)	DESIGN OF MAN–COMPUTER DIALOGUES
APPLICATION DEVELOPMENT WITHOUT PROGRAMMERS	TELEMATIC SOCIETY	VIEWDATA AND THE INFORMATION SOCIETY